BARNES & NOBLE BASICS™

in the
Kitchen

by Pamela Richards

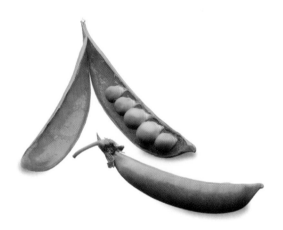

Formerly published as
I'm in the Kitchen, Now What?!

**BARNES
&NOBLE**
B O O K S

For information, contact:
Silver Lining Books
122 Fifth Avenue
New York, NY 10011
212-633-4000

introduction

KELLY MILLER WAS NERVOUS. FOUR GUESTS WERE DUE TO arrive for dinner in an hour. Could she possibly pull it off? Serve a great dinner, that is. "I was all set to go. I just had to do the last step for the main dish. But the recipe said something about reducing the sauce. What did that mean? How do you do that? Okay, I panicked and picked up the telephone and ordered in."

Sound familiar? Small wonder. Cooking can be a perilous adventure. It doesn't help that so many recipes are written by cooking professionals who have forgotten the fear and anxiety of starting out. That's where Barnes & Noble Basics *In the Kitchen* comes in. It is written by Pamela Richards, a cooking teacher for beginners, who knows how to dispel the anxiety most novice cooks feel upon entering the kitchen. Every recipe is broken down into steps and is written in simple, easy-to-follow language. Every recipe gives detailed instructions for procedures and techniques so that nothing is left to chance. Substitutions are right there. And every recipe anticipates every cook's questions. We're talking superlative driving instructions here! So crank up your stove and put on your mitts. There are some fabulous recipes waiting for you! Enjoy the journey.

Barb Chintz
Editorial Director, the **Barnes & Noble Basics**™ series

contents

kitchen essentials

Having the right equipment on hand takes a huge amount of stress out of cooking. Here are the basics you will need to get started right.

EQUIPMENT

large saucepan

small saucepan

roasting pan

skillet

stockpot

Dutch oven

mixer

blender

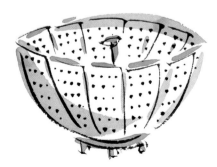

steamer

PREPARATION

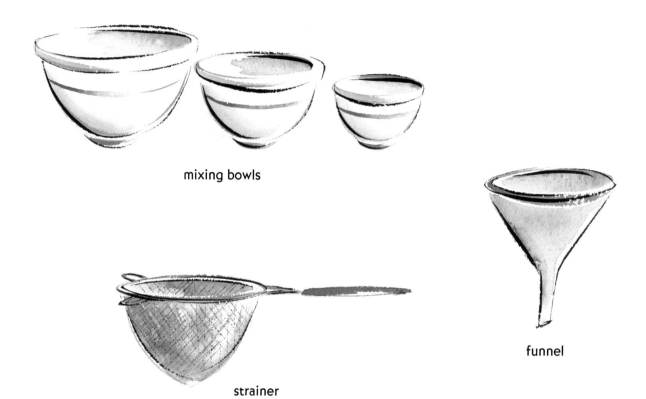

mixing bowls

strainer

funnel

colander

BAKING

pie pan

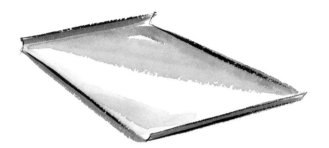

baking sheet

baking dish

MEASURES

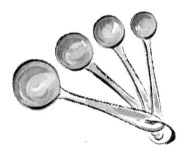

measuring spoons

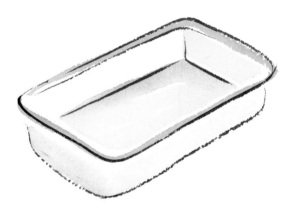

dry measures

measuring cup

TOOLS

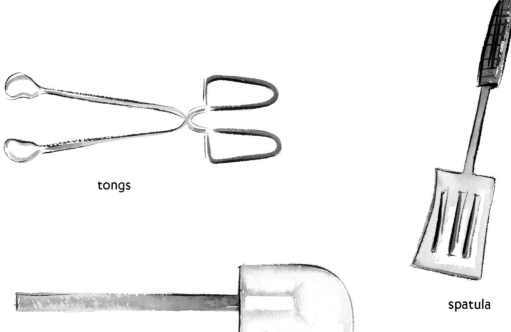

tongs

spatula

rubber spatula

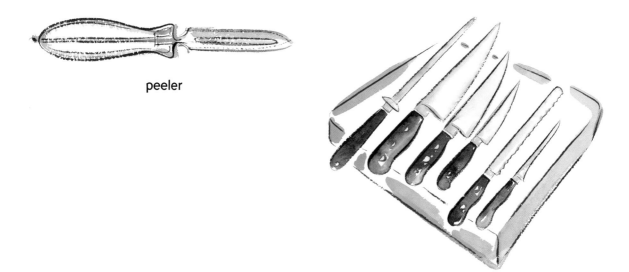

peeler

knives with knife sharpener

slotted spoon

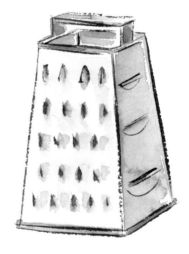

whisk

wooden spoon

grater

pastry brush

1 Appetizers

Tempt your guests with these delicious offerings: Baked Spinach Balls (top), Guacamole (middle), and Cheese-Filled Phyllo Shells (bottom).

mushroom pâté

A New Age pâté, served chilled with a nice red wine—a Merlot or Pinot Noir—is sublime

Serves 6-8 ✻ *Prep time: 20 minutes* ✻ *Cooking time: 10 minutes*
✻ *Chilling time: 2 hours*

INGREDIENTS

- **4½ tablespoons** butter, softened
- **½ pound** mushrooms, cleaned and minced
- **1 teaspoon** minced shallots
- **1 teaspoon** minced garlic
- **¼ cup** minced scallions
- **⅓ cup** low-sodium chicken broth
- **¼ cup** minced walnuts
- **½ teaspoon** lemon juice
- **4 ounces** light cream cheese, softened
- **1 teaspoon** salt
- **1 teaspoon** black pepper

1. MELT 2 tablespoons of butter in medium-size skillet over medium heat. Add mushrooms, shallots, garlic and scallions and cook for 2 to 3 minutes, stirring occasionally.

2. ADD the chicken broth to the skillet and cook over medium heat until all the liquid has been absorbed, about 4 to 5 minutes. (It will bubble slightly.) Add the walnuts and lemon juice and stir to combine. Take the skillet off the stove and let mixture cool for about 20 minutes.

3. COMBINE cream cheese and remaining 2½ tablespoons of butter in a mixing bowl. Add the mushroom mixture and combine. Stir in salt and pepper and mix well.

4. FILL a 1-cup crockery bowl (or whatever pretty dish you have) with the mushroom mixture, and smooth surface. Cover with plastic wrap and refrigerate for at least two hours so flavors can meld.

5. SERVE with crackers or toast points (white toast cut into triangles), or, for easy elegance, endive leaves.

easy bruschetta

Goat cheese and white beans accentuate this traditional Italian appetizer—fresh basil is key

Serves 8-10 ✳ *Prep time: 20 minutes* ✳ *Cooking time: 8 minutes*

INGREDIENTS

- **1 can (15.5 ounces)** small white beans, rinsed and drained
- **5** plum tomatoes, coarsely chopped, or **5** canned plum tomatoes, chopped
- **½ cup** minced onion
- **½ cup** fresh basil, rinsed and minced, or **2 tablespoons** dried basil
- **3 cloves** garlic, minced
- **1½ tablespoons** balsamic vinegar
- **4 tablespoons** olive oil
- Black pepper, to taste
- **1** long loaf Italian bread or French baguette, cut into ½-inch-thick slices
- **6 ounces** mild goat cheese, softened

1. PREHEAT oven to 375°F.

2. In a medium-size mixing bowl, **COMBINE** white beans, tomatoes, onion, basil, garlic, balsamic vinegar, and 2 tablespoons of the olive oil. Season with black pepper, to taste.

3. Place bread on large baking sheet and **BRUSH** with the remaining 2 tablespoons of olive oil using a pastry brush. (If you don't have a pastry brush, use the back of a spoon to smooth the oil over the bread.) **BAKE** until bread is toasted and golden brown, about 8 to 10 minutes. Watch the oven so the bread doesn't burn!

4. REMOVE bread from the oven and spread the softened goat cheese over each slice. **TOP** with tomato-bean mixture.

5. SERVE immediately.

sun-dried tomatoes and cheese terrine

So pretty to look at, so scrumptious to eat when spread on crackers or pita bread

Serves 16 ✳ *Prep time: 20 minutes* ✳ *Cooking time: none*

INGREDIENTS

- **3 cups** grated Fontina cheese
- **12 ounces** reduced-fat cream cheese, softened
- **8 ounces** mild goat cheese
- **2 cups** prepared or home-made (see page 140) pesto
- **2 cups** sun-dried tomatoes, refreshed, drained, and minced (see next page)
- **1½ cups** pine nuts, lightly toasted

1. LINE a 9 x 5 x 3-inch **loaf pan** with plastic wrap, draping the wrap over the sides and ends of the pan. (It's just like lining a shoe box with tissue paper.)

2. SPREAD one cup of the Fontina cheese on bottom of prepared pan, covering entire surface.

3. In a small bowl, use a fork to **COMBINE** the cream cheese and goat cheese, mixing thoroughly.

4. SPREAD half of the cream cheese mixture over the Fontina cheese layer.

5. SPREAD half of the pesto over the cream cheese layer.

6. SPREAD half of the sun-dried tomatoes over the pesto layer.

7. SPRINKLE half of the toasted pine nuts over the tomato layer. Press down lightly with your hands.

8. SPRINKLE one cup of the Fontina over the pine nuts.

9. REPEAT all layers, ending with a layer of the remaining Fontina cheese on top. Your loaf will be about 3 inches high.

10. FOLD plastic wrap over surface of cheese and cover pan with aluminum foil. Refrigerate terrine until ready to serve, or freeze for up to one month. To defrost, remove from freezer and let stand at room temperature for about 8 hours.

11. When ready to serve, **UNWRAP** loaf pan and invert the pan onto a platter. Lift pan up and remove foil and plastic wrap. Voilà, a gorgeous thing! Serve with crackers or pita bread that has been cut into small bite-size triangles.

✳ NOW WHAT?! ✳

🔵 **Whenever I grate cheese, it always sticks to the grater. How do I avoid this mess?** Spray your grater with nonstick vegetable spray before grating cheese, and the cleanup will be a breeze! If you are grating several foods, save messy items like cheese for last. It also helps if you grate cheese when it's cold.

• • •

🔵 **What's the best way to clean cheese off my grater?** Use an old (but clean!) toothbrush to clean your grater— it's the perfect tool.

WHAT IS IT AND WHERE DO I FIND IT?

SUN-DRIED TOMATOES are usually dried in the sun, resulting in a chewy, intensely flavored, sweet-dark-red tomato. You can buy them dry, packed in oil, or in paste form. Dry-packed tomatoes are far less expensive than those packed in oil (it's the oil you're paying for!), and the only disadvantage is that they must be refreshed, or rehydrated, before they can be used. All you have to do to refresh them is place them in a bowl, cover them with boiling water, and let them stand for about 15 minutes. Drain them, then pat dry with paper towels before using.

• • •

FONTINA is a semifirm cow's-milk cheese from Italy. It resembles Gruyère but is softer and has a richer taste.

• • •

PESTO is a wonderful herb sauce made from basil, pine nuts, olive oil, and Parmesan cheese. It's available premade and is sold in plastic containers in the specialty-food section of most supermarkets. To make your own, see page 140.

unfried chicken fingers

This is a super-quick, healthy appetizer that even little kids will devour

Yields 20 fingers ✳ *Prep time: 30 minutes* ✳ *Cooking time: 12-15 minutes*

INGREDIENTS

1 ½ **pounds** skinless, boneless chicken breasts or chicken tenders

2 egg whites, lightly beaten

1 ½ **tablespoons** honey

2 ½ **cups** crushed cornflakes

½ **teaspoon** black pepper

1 **teaspoon** garlic powder

SAUCE

⅓ **cup** honey

3 **tablespoons** Dijon mustard

4 **ounces** apricot preserves

½ **teaspoon** garlic powder

1 ½ **teaspoons** soy sauce

¼ **cup** water

for the chicken

1. **PREHEAT** oven to 450°F.

2. **RINSE** chicken and pat dry with paper towels. (This is vital—don't skip it.) Cut chicken into strips that are 3 inches long by ¾ inches wide, so that they look like fingers. You should have about 20 to 25 strips.

3. **COMBINE** egg whites and honey in a small mixing bowl.

4. **MIX** crushed cornflakes, pepper, and garlic powder in a shallow bowl.

5. **DIP** chicken strips into the egg white mixture, then roll each strip in the crumb mixture to coat.

6. **PLACE** chicken fingers in a single layer on an ungreased baking sheet.

7. **BAKE** chicken in oven for 12 to 15 minutes or until juices run clear when pierced with a fork. Don't worry about turning the fingers—it's not necessary.

for the sauce

1. In a medium-size saucepan, **STIR** together the honey, mustard, apricot preserves, garlic powder, soy sauce, and water over medium-low heat. Stirring often, cook until the preserves are just melted, about 2 to 3 minutes. Transfer into a small dish and serve as a dipping sauce for the chicken fingers. (If you are short on time, use a prepared honey-mustard sauce.)

☀ **NOW WHAT?!** ☀

I hate cutting up chicken. Is there an easy way? Yes. Use poultry shears or other all-purpose kitchen scissors to cut up chicken. They're often much easier to use than a knife—particularly a dull one!

• • •

Is raw chicken safe? I'm worried about salmonella. Bacteria! Bacteria! Bacteria! It flourishes in poultry at temperatures between 40° F and 140° F, so DO NOT let chicken sit out on your counter for too long before cooking. Bacteria that lives on raw poultry can contaminate any food it comes in contact with, so it's vital to use hot, soapy water to thoroughly wash your hands, work surface, and utensils after preparing poultry.

FIRST PERSON DISASTER

Getting Plastered

I saw this great recipe for chicken and was really keen to try it. The recipe called for rolling the chicken pieces in flour and spices and then sautéing it in chicken broth. What could be easier? Especially since a bag of flour was already there on the kitchen counter. I prepared the chicken, cooked it with some vegetables, and called everyone in for dinner. There was only one problem—we couldn't cut into the chicken. It was as if it were encased in plaster. My son started to chuckle. "Mom, did you use the plaster of Paris I left on the counter?" I nodded. "Didn't you always tell us to check the ingredients first?" I nodded again and added, "Remember: Do what I say, not what I do."

Sally M., New York, New York

nacho cheese dip

A creamy dip with just a dash of jalapeño—use tortilla chips to scoop it up

Serves 10 ✳ *Prep time: 15 minutes* ✳ *Cooking time: 10 minutes*

INGREDIENTS

- ¾ **cup** beer
- 1 ½ **teaspoons** ground cumin
- ½ **teaspoon** ground coriander
- 1 **teaspoon** dried oregano
- 1 **teaspoon** garlic powder
- 1 **can** (**16 ounces**) refried beans
- 1 ½ **cups** ready-made salsa (medium or hot)
- 1 **teaspoon** minced canned or fresh jalapeño peppers
- 1 ½ **packages** (**24 ounces**) Velveeta cheese, cut into 1-inch pieces
- 1 **tablespoon** dried cilantro or parsley, or ½ **cup** chopped fresh cilantro

Tortilla chips

1. COMBINE beer, cumin, coriander, oregano, and garlic powder in a medium saucepan. Heat over low heat and bring to a simmer (you'll see pearl-size bubbles forming). Add beans, salsa, and jalapeños and stir until heated through. Add Velveeta and stir until cheese melts, about 3 to 4 minutes. Stir in cilantro. Transfer to a bowl and serve with tortilla chips. Reheat as needed.

WHAT IS IT AND WHERE DO I FIND IT?

JALAPEÑO PEPPERS are small (2 to 3 inches long), but they are packed with hot, spicy flavor. They are dark green and quite hot, and they're available fresh (look for them in the produce section of your supermarket) or canned, whole or already chopped. The more jalapeños you use, the spicier the dip!

• • •

VELVEETA CHEESE, as used in this dip, lets you relive the past. Yes, Velveeta is that orange stuff in the big rectangular box from days gone by. But it still makes a fabulous warm dipping sauce, smooth as velvet (hence the name). Better yet, it doesn't curdle (separate) when heated.

white bean hummus

Use white beans instead of chickpeas for a sweeter, lighter hummus

Serves 10 ✳ *Prep time: 15 minutes* ✳ *Cooking time: none*

INGREDIENTS

- **I** **can (15.5 ounces)** small white beans, rinsed and drained
- **3** **tablespoons** lemon juice
- ¼ **cup** chopped red onion (about half an onion)
- **3** **cloves** garlic, peeled
- ¼ **teaspoon** ground cumin
- ¼ **teaspoon** salt
- ½ **teaspoon** black pepper
- **I** **teaspoon** dried parsley or **2 tablespoons** chopped fresh parsley

Pita bread triangles

Mini carrots, raw

I. PLACE everything except the parsley, pita bread, and carrots in a blender or the bowl of a food processor fitted with a steel blade and process until smooth. Spoon the hummus into a serving bowl and garnish with chopped parsley.

2. SERVE with pita triangles and raw carrots.

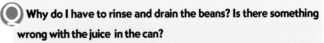

✳ **NOW WHAT?!** ✳

🔘 **Why do I have to rinse and drain the beans? Is there something wrong with the juice in the can?**

No. It's just that those juices are loaded with salt. You need to rinse them off, or the taste of your recipe will be distorted.

baked spinach balls

A delicious and healthful way to start a party

Serves 6 ✳ *Prep time: 15 minutes* ✳ *Cooking time: 12 minutes*

INGREDIENTS

- **1 box (10 ounces)** frozen chopped spinach
- **¼ cup** minced shallots
- **2** extra-large egg whites, lightly beaten
- **½ cup** plain bread crumbs
- **¼ cup** plus **2 tablespoons** grated Parmesan cheese
- **1 ½ tablespoons** lemon juice
- **½ teaspoon** salt
- **½ teaspoon** black pepper

YOGURT DIP

- **½ cup** plain low-fat yogurt
- **1 teaspoon** dried dill or **3 teaspoons** chopped fresh dill
- **1 ½ teaspoons** garlic paste or **1 teaspoon** garlic powder

1. PREHEAT oven to 400°F.

2. MICROWAVE spinach according to package instructions. Drain spinach, cool, and wring it dry (see the amazing tip on the next page).

3. COMBINE the spinach, shallots, egg whites, bread crumbs, Parmesan, lemon juice, salt, and pepper in a medium-size bowl.

4. ROLL the spinach mixture into 1-inch balls. How? Just put a little in your hand and roll into a ball as you would clay. Place the balls on a baking sheet that has been greased with vegetable oil or sprayed with vegetable oil cooking spray. Bake on the middle rack of the oven for 12 minutes. The balls should be slightly golden brown. Serve immediately with yogurt dip on the side.

for the dip

1. COMBINE the yogurt, dill, and garlic in a small bowl, mixing well with a fork.

2. SERVE the spinach balls with the dip.

Bite-size morsels of spinach
with a refreshing yogurt-dill dip

✳ **NOW WHAT?!** ✳

◉ **How do I dry spinach?**

The best way to squeeze all the water out of spinach is to place it in a clean dish towel or—believe it or not—into the foot of a clean knee-high stocking and wring dry. You'll spend too much time and effort trying to get the water out using any other method!

guacamole

Avocados and a fabulous blend of spices and garlic make a superb guacamole every time

Serves 6-8 ✳ *Prep time: 15 minutes* ✳ *Cooking time: None*

INGREDIENTS

- **4** ripe Haas avocados
- **3 tablespoons** lemon juice
- **3 tablespoons** lime juice
- **1** large tomato, minced
- **¼ cup** onion, minced
- **2 cloves** garlic, minced
- **2 teaspoons** black pepper
- **1 teaspoon** salt
- **5-10 dashes** Tabasco
- **1 ½ teaspoons** dried parsley or **2 tablespoons** chopped fresh cilantro or parsley
- **Large** bag of tortilla chips

1. SLICE each avocado in half; remove and discard the pits. Using a large spoon, scoop the meat into a medium-size bowl. Add the lemon and lime juices.

2. MASH avocado with back side of a fork until slightly chunky, mixing it with the lemon and lime juices.

3. CHOP the tomato into ¼-inch pieces.

4. ADD tomato and the remaining ingredients to the avocado mixture and mix until just combined. Yields about 3 cups.

5. SERVE with tortilla chips.

WHAT IS IT AND WHERE DO I FIND IT?

HAAS AVOCADO: Once upon a time, there was an alligator pear, better known as the Haas avocado that we love today. True, it looks ugly and bumpy on the outside, but its flesh is buttery and irresistible! The other variety you can find in the market, which has a shiny skin and far less flavor, is known as the Fuerte.

How do I keep avocados, and hence guacamole, green?

Avocado flesh is a lovely shade of green, but it turns brown when exposed to air. To retard browning, brush the avocado surface with lemon or lime juice. The faster you add lemon or lime juice to your guacamole, the less likely that it will turn brown. (It's the acid in the juice that slows the browning and brightens the flavor.) Once you have combined all of the guacamole ingredients, press plastic wrap directly onto the dip (make sure the wrap and dip touch) in order to maintain its color.

* * *

How do I know if my avocado is ripe?

By the time most people have finished testing for ripeness, the avocado is so bruised that it's no longer worth using! To check for ripeness, hold the fruit in your hand. If it yields slightly to gentle pressure from your palm, it is ripe. In other words, if it gives a little, it's ready for consumption. Be careful not to squeeze it too much, as you'll induce bad spots. If it's hard, take it home and wait a few days until it ripens. If you're in a hurry, save yourself a day by wrapping the avocado in aluminum foil. (Microwaving will only soften the avocado, not ripen it.)

Nothing disappears
faster than flavorful,
homemade guacamole.

spinach dip

Sure, onion dip is fine, but why not try something a little more elegant? No cooking required

Serves 6 ✳ *Prep time: 10 minutes* ✳ *Cooking time: none*

INGREDIENTS

1 large round peasant bread

⅓ **cup** extra-virgin olive oil

2 **boxes (10 ounces** each) frozen spinach, thawed and drained

2½ **tablespoons** lemon juice

3 **cloves** garlic, chopped

Salt and black pepper to taste

Crackers (optional)

1. CUT a ½-inch-thick slice of bread and place it on a plate. Pour 3 tablespoons of olive oil over it, turning it to coat completely. Let the bread stand in the oil until it has absorbed it (about 5 minutes), then tear the bread into pieces.

2. In a blender or the bowl of a food processor fitted with a steel blade, **ADD** the spinach and blend until smooth. Add the bread, lemon juice, and garlic and blend or process until smooth. Add the remaining olive oil and purée the mixture. Season with salt and pepper and spoon into a bowl. Note: Dip will be runny. Serve with thin slices of warm, crusty peasant bread or crackers.

✳ **WHAT IS IT AND WHERE DO I FIND IT?** ✳

PEASANT BREAD is the down-home name for any round loaf of white bread that is crusty on the outside. It is anywhere from 5 to 10 inches in diameter and is available at large supermarkets, specialty food shops, and bakeries.

cheese and bacon puffs

These are great with serious cocktails or a lovely chilled Chardonnay

Yields 30 puffs ✳ *Prep time: 15 minutes* ✳ *Cooking time: 10 minutes*

INGREDIENTS

- **1 pound** cooked, crisp bacon, crumbled
- **1 cup** mayonnaise
- **1 cup** grated sharp cheddar cheese
- **4** scallions, thinly sliced (white and green parts)
- **2 tablespoons** dry sherry
- **1 teaspoon** white Worcestershire sauce (optional)
- **3 drops** Tabasco (or other hot sauce)

Melba rounds

1. FRY the bacon in a skillet or cook it in a microwave until crisp—crisp bacon crumbles more easily. (To microwave: Separate the strips and place 6 at a time on a paper towel. Roll up the paper towel and place in the microwave; cook on high for 2 to 3 minutes. Continue with another set of strips on a new piece of towel.) Set bacon aside so it can cool, overnight if you wish, then chop it into ¼-inch pieces or crumble it with your fingers.

2. MIX all ingredients in a bowl and chill for 3 hours or overnight. (The mixture will keep for as long as three days if refrigerated, in case you want to prepare it ahead of time.)

when ready to serve

3. PREHEAT broiler. Note: Before you turn the oven on, make sure the upper rack is about 5 inches from the broiler coils.

4. SPREAD mixture on melba rounds and place on a cookie sheet. Put the cookie sheet on the oven rack and broil until the cheese is bubbly, only 2 to 3 minutes.

5. SERVE immediately.

cheese-filled phyllo shells

Ready-made phyllo shells make this sumptuous appetizer so easy to prepare

Yields 45 ✳ *Prep time: 20 minutes* ✳ *Cooking time: 10 minutes*

INGREDIENTS

- **3 boxes** frozen phyllo shells
- **⅔ cup** grated Parmesan cheese
- **½ pound** mozzarella cheese, grated
- **¾ pound** light cream cheese, softened
- **2** eggs, lightly beaten
- **1 cup** refreshed sun-dried tomatoes, chopped (see page 17)
- **1 cup** fresh basil leaves, washed, dried, and minced, or **2 tablespoons** dried basil
- **3 cloves** garlic, minced

Salt and black pepper to taste

1. PREHEAT oven to 350°F. Remove the phyllo shells from their boxes and place on an ungreased baking or cookie sheet. Shells will thaw in about 10 minutes.

2. MIX together cheeses, eggs, tomatoes, basil, garlic, salt, and pepper in large bowl.

3. FILL each phyllo shell with mixture, mounding slightly.

4. BAKE in oven for 8 to 10 minutes or until mixture begins to bubble. Remove shells from baking sheet and place on serving platter. Serve warm.

WHAT IS IT AND WHERE DO I FIND IT?

PHYLLO SHELLS come 15 to a box and are available in the freezer section of most grocery stores. They should be near the frozen pie crusts and phyllo sheets.

Phyllo shells (shown cooked, inset) turn an ordinary filling of cheese and sun-dried tomatoes into an elegant treat.

2 Soups

Too inviting not to try: Carrot-Ginger Soup (top), White Bean and Spinach Soup (middle), and Chicken Noodle Soup (bottom)

chicken noodle soup

Put leftover chicken to good use with this delicious, hearty soup

Serves 6 ✳ *Prep time: 20 minutes* ✳ *Cooking time: 35 minutes*

INGREDIENTS

- **1 teaspoon** olive oil
- **1 cup** chopped onions
- **1½ teaspoons** dried oregano
- **1 teaspoon** dried basil
- **2 cloves** garlic, minced
- **8 cups** low-sodium chicken stock (canned or homemade —see page 50)
- **1 cup** peeled, diced potato
- **1½ cups** chopped celery
- **1½ cups** sliced carrots
- **3½ cups** shredded cooked chicken (white meat only)
- **2 boxes (10 ounces** each) frozen chopped spinach, thawed and drained
- **1¼ teaspoons** salt
- **1-2 teaspoons** black pepper
- **6 ounces** uncooked egg noodles (thin ones)
- **2 tablespoons** all-purpose flour

1. HEAT the oil in a large, heavy soup pot over medium heat.

2. ADD the onions and cook over medium-high heat (turning the onions frequently so they won't burn) for about 3 minutes or until they are translucent.

3. ADD the oregano, basil, and garlic and sauté 1 minute. (Cooking the herbs in oil brings out more of their flavor.)

4. ADD 7½ cups of the chicken stock. Increase the heat, bringing the mixture to a **BOIL** (nickel-size bubbles will form every few seconds). Add the potato.

5. REDUCE the heat and **SIMMER** (pearl-size bubbles will form every few seconds). Cook uncovered for 15 minutes, stirring occasionally.

6. Using a potato masher or the back of a large spoon, **MASH** the potato into the stock. The soup should look a little cloudy. (This is the trick to thickening the soup.)

7. ADD the celery, carrots, chicken, spinach, salt, and pepper and return to a boil. Reduce the heat and simmer 5 to 6 minutes.

8. ADD the noodles, return to a boil, and cook 5 minutes or until the noodles are tender.

9. While the noodles are cooking, **WHISK** together ½ cup stock and flour in a small bowl. (This mixture is called a slurry. It looks a bit like goopy wallpaper paste, but its purpose is quite elegant: It slightly thickens the soup.) Whisk several tablespoons of the broth into the slurry, then stir the mixture into the soup. Simmer for 3 to 4 minutes.

10. LADLE the soup into warmed bowls and serve.

☀ **NOW WHAT?!** ☀

🔵 **What's the best way to avoid adding too much salt or pepper?**
Add both salt and pepper gradually, about ¼ teaspoon at a time, tasting as you go.

• • •

🔵 **What should I do if I add too much salt?**
Add a peeled, thinly sliced raw potato to the pot and simmer the soup for 10 to 15 minutes. Remove the potato before serving the soup, or chop it up and mix it into the soup.

down east clam chowder

The real deal—clams in their shells in the soup

Serves 6 ✳ *Prep time: 20 minutes* ✳ *Cooking time: 30 minutes*

INGREDIENTS

- **3 tablespoons** butter
- **4** small leeks, washed and thinly sliced
- **2 cloves** garlic, minced
- ¼ **cup** flour
- **3 cups** whole milk
- **3 bottles** (**8 ounces** each) clam juice
- 1⅔ **pounds** russet potatoes, peeled and cut into ½-inch cubes
- Salt and pepper to taste
- Littleneck clams (**4½ pounds** fresh, the shells well scrubbed) or **3 cans** (**8 ounces** each)

1. In a large, heavy pot, **MELT** the butter over medium heat until just liquid but not yet turning brown. Add the leeks and garlic and cook over medium-high heat for 3 minutes, turning the mixture frequently so that it doesn't burn.

2. ADD the flour and stir with a spoon for about 2 minutes.

3. Gradually **MIX** in the milk and clam juice, preferably using a whisk.

4. INCREASE the heat to high, bringing the mixture to a boil (nickel-size bubbles will form every few seconds). Add the potatoes.

5. REDUCE the heat to low and cook soup, uncovered, for about 15 minutes, stirring occasionally. Season to taste with salt and pepper.

6. ADD the clams, leaving them in their shells. Simmer for another 4 to 5 minutes, or until the clams open.

7. LADLE the chowder into bowls and serve.

🔘 **Whenever I make chowder, my clams get tough. Why does this happen?**

The key to chowder is to not cook it too long—the flavor gets too strong and the clams toughen up. If you remove the soup from the heat promptly when the clams open, the resulting flavor will be gentle and the clams will remain tender.

• • •

🔘 **How do I tell if a clam is bad?**

When you select clams, make sure the shells are tightly closed. If they appear slightly open, rap them with your knuckles. If they don't close, toss them out—they are either dead or dying.

• • •

🔘 **Can I use canned clams for this recipe?**

Yes, but their texture will be different from that of fresh ones. You will need 1½ pounds of canned clams or 3 cans (8 ounces each).

• • •

🔘 **How do I eat the clams in the soup?**

Some of the clams will fall out of their shells and into the soup; some will fall out after they have been ladled into a bowl. Eat those with your spoon. The ones that remain in the shell will require a little effort. Scoop out a clam shell with your spoon, then use your fingers to dig out the clam. Who said you shouldn't eat with your fingers?

sherried mushroom soup

A silky, flavorful first course or light supper with bread and salad

Serves 6 ✳ *Prep time: 15 minutes* ✳ *Cooking time: 35 minutes*

INGREDIENTS

3 tablespoons butter

1¼ cups chopped onions

2½ pounds portobello and shiitake mushrooms, thinly sliced (see next page)

5 cups low-sodium chicken broth (canned or home-made—see page 50)

⅓ cup dry sherry (see note)

Salt and black pepper, to taste

¼ cup heavy cream or evaporated skim milk

1. In a large, heavy saucepan, **MELT** the butter over medium heat until it is liquid and not yet turning brown.

2. **ADD** the onions and cook over medium-high heat for 5 minutes, turning frequently.

3. **ADD** the mushrooms and cook for about 8 to 10 minutes, until the mushrooms have softened and the liquid they give off has evaporated.

4. **ADD** the chicken broth. Reduce the heat and simmer uncovered (pearl-size bubbles will form every few seconds) for 15 minutes.

5. **REMOVE** the soup from the heat and allow it to cool for 5 minutes. Pour half the soup into a blender and purée. Pour the puréed mixture back into the chunky portion of soup.

6. **ADD** the sherry, salt, pepper, and cream; stir to combine. Heat the soup for a few minutes until it's hot, stirring constantly to prevent curdling.

7. **LADLE** the soup into bowls and serve.

Why do mushrooms always become mushy after I wash them?

Clean mushrooms just before you cook them, and never immerse them in water—mushrooms are extremely absorbent (much like a sponge) and will become mushy. The best solution is to rinse them in a colander under cold running water, then immediately blot them dry with a paper towel.

• • •

Is it necessary to sauté the mushrooms before making the soup?

Yes, sautéing the mushrooms concentrates and releases their flavor. Don't crowd them all into the pan—you want to be able to stir them around. If the temperature is not high enough or the mushrooms are crowded, they will steam instead of sauté, and will not be as flavorful.

WHAT IS IT AND WHERE DO I FIND IT?

MUSHROOMS come in many varieties, and most are available in grocery stores. If the large brown portobello or black Japanese shiitake mushrooms are not available near you, ask for chanterelle, morel, or porcini mushrooms. Look for the firm, straight gills which indicate that a mushroom is fresh. (Remove the large stems for this recipe.) Use mushrooms soon after you purchase them—they don't keep well after 4 days.

• • •

SHERRY is a fortified wine that comes in three styles: dry, sweet, and cream. For cooking purposes, get a good dry sherry such as Amontillado. It will add tremendous flavor to your food. Once opened, a bottle of sherry will keep for up to one year.

carrot-ginger soup

The zippy tang of fresh ginger combines with the
sweetness of carrots to create a superb soup

Serves 6 ✳ *Prep time: 20 minutes* ✳ *Cooking time: 35 minutes*

INGREDIENTS

- **3 tablespoons** vegetable oil
- **2** leeks, washed and minced (white parts only)
- **¼ cup** peeled, minced fresh ginger or **1 tablespoon** ground ginger
- **4 cups** low-sodium chicken broth (canned or home-made—see page 50)
- **1 ½ pounds** carrots, peeled and sliced (about **4 cups**)
- **1 cup** orange juice
- **½ cup** half-and-half
- **½ teaspoon** ground cinnamon
- **½ teaspoon** ground cardamom
- **1 teaspoon** salt
- **1 ¼ teaspoons** black pepper
- **Garnish** (optional): chopped fresh parsley

1. HEAT the oil in a large, heavy saucepan. Add the leeks and ginger and cook over medium-high heat, turning the mixture frequently so that it doesn't burn, about 5 minutes.

2. ADD chicken broth and carrots. Increase the heat to high and bring the mixture to a **BOIL** (nickel-size bubbles will form every few seconds). Reduce the heat to low so that the mixture **SIMMERS** (pearl-size bubbles will form every few seconds). Cover the pot and cook until the carrots are tender, about 20 minutes.

3. REMOVE the soup from the heat and let it stand for 5 minutes. Then purée the soup in batches in a blender. Return the puréed mixture to the saucepan.

4. STIR in the orange juice, half-and-half, cinnamon, cardamom, salt, and pepper and simmer uncovered for 5 minutes.

5. LADLE the soup into bowls, garnish with parsley (if desired), and serve.

🔘 **Why do I have to bring the soup to a boil first, then immediately lower the heat and simmer?**

The initial boiling helps bring out the flavors. Simmering the soup afterward does not reduce the liquid, but simply finishes the cooking process.

Carrot-ginger soup served with hot, crusty bread is the perfect meal for a cool autumn day.

WHAT IS IT AND WHERE DO I FIND IT?

GINGER is a knobby root vegetable that can be found in the produce section of most supermarkets. Buy only smooth ginger—if it is cracked or wrinkled, it's past its prime. Use a vegetable peeler to remove the thin, brown skin, but be sure to peel only the skin, as the delicate flesh just under the surface is the most flavorful. One tablespoon of ground ginger can be used instead of $1/4$ cup fresh ginger.

butternut squash soup

A true fall classic—earthy-flavored and golden-hued

Serves 4-6 ✳ *Prep time: 15 minutes* ✳ *Cooking time: 30 minutes*

INGREDIENTS

- **4 tablespoons** butter
- **1 tablespoon** vegetable oil
- **1 medium** Spanish onion, chopped
- **1** leek, washed and minced (white and light-green parts, only)
- **2 pounds** butternut squash, peeled, seeded, and cut into 1-inch pieces
- **4-5 cups** low-sodium chicken broth (canned or homemade, see page 50)
- **¼ teaspoon** ground nutmeg
- **1 teaspoon** salt
- **1 teaspoon** black pepper
- **⅓ cup** evaporated skim milk
- **Garnish** (optional): Chopped parsley or dill (fresh or dried)

1. In a large, heavy saucepan, **MELT** the butter over medium heat for about 2 minutes, until it's liquid but not yet turning brown. Add the oil to the butter and stir together with a whisk or spoon.

2. ADD the onion and leek and cook over medium-high heat for 5 to 6 minutes, turning them frequently so they don't burn.

3. ADD the squash and cook for 5 minutes.

4. ADD 4 cups of broth and the nutmeg to the pot. Reduce the heat to medium-low and **SIMMER** (pearl-size bubbles will form every few seconds) for 15 to 20 minutes or until the squash is tender enough to pierce with a fork.

5. REMOVE the soup from the heat and let it cool for 5 minutes. Purée the soup in batches in a blender. Return the soup to the saucepan and stir in the salt, pepper, and evaporated milk. (If soup is too thick, thin it by adding more broth, a few tablespoons at a time. Rewarm the soup on low heat and taste it for seasoning—add more salt and pepper as desired.)

6. LADLE the soup into individual bowls and garnish with parsley or dill. Serve.

WHAT IS IT AND WHERE DO I FIND IT?

BUTTERNUT SQUASH is a winter squash that is 6 to 9 inches tall with a bulbous base and hard, light-brown skin. Before cooking, cut it in half, remove the seeds from the center, and discard. To make peeling the skin easier, microwave the squash on high for 1 to 2 minutes, then let it stand for a few minutes longer. Use a sharp knife or vegetable peeler to remove the skin.

* * *

EVAPORATED MILK: Think of it as thick milk in a can. Essentially, it's regular milk with about 60 percent of the water removed. It's a cook's secret weapon: Just open it and pour into dishes that require cream—creamed soups, vegetables in cream sauce, gravies. Evaporated milk comes in whole, low-fat, and skimmed versions. It's sold in cans and, unlike sweetened condensed milk, is not sweet. You can find it in the baking section of your supermarket. Keep a few cans in the pantry—they come in handy for enriching last-minute meals.

☀ NOW WHAT?! ☀

Can I use sweetened condensed milk instead of evaporated milk?
No! It will not work. Evaporated milk is not sweetened, while sweetened condensed milk is about 40 percent sugar—the sweetness will ruin the earthy flavor of the soup.

turkey and black bean soup

Turn leftover turkey into a fiesta!

Serves 6 ✸ *Prep time: 20 minutes* ✸ *Cooking time: 45 minutes*

INGREDIENTS

- **2 tablespoons** canola or vegetable oil
- **1 ¼ cups** chopped red onion
- **1 ¼ cups** chopped carrot
- **1 cup** chopped celery
- **4 cloves** garlic, minced
- **1 ½ tablespoons** ground cumin
- **1 teaspoon** dried oregano
- **½ teaspoon** dried coriander
- **4 cups** low-sodium chicken broth (canned or homemade, see page 50)
- **2 ¼ cups** water
- **1 teaspoon** salt
- **2 cans (15.5 ounces each)** black beans, drained
- **1 pound** turkey breasts, cooked and coarsely chopped
- **1** red bell pepper, cut into ½-inch pieces
- **2 teaspoons** dried parsley
- **¼ cup** dry sherry (see page 37)

1. HEAT the oil in a large pot over medium heat. Add the onion, carrot, celery, garlic, cumin, oregano, and coriander. Cook over medium heat for 5 minutes, stirring constantly so the food doesn't burn.

2. ADD the broth, water, salt, and beans and stir to combine. Increase the heat to high and bring the mixture to a **BOIL** (nickel-size bubbles will form every few seconds). Reduce the heat to low so that the mixture **SIMMERS** (pearl-size bubbles will form every few seconds). Cook for 20 to 25 minutes or until vegetables are just tender enough to be pierced with a fork.

3. REMOVE the bean mixture from the heat and let it cool for 10 minutes. Transfer half of the bean mixture to a blender and purée until smooth. Return the purée to the remaining chunky bean mixture and stir to combine.

4. ADD the cooked turkey. Stir in the bell pepper, dried parsley, and sherry. Cook the mixture for 5 minutes over medium-low heat, stirring until thoroughly heated.

5. LADLE the soup into bowls and serve.

Storage tip: This soup can be frozen in an airtight plastic container for up to three months (after that, the texture begins to degrade). To thaw soup, reheat it over medium-low heat, stirring frequently.

WHAT IS IT AND WHERE DO I FIND IT?

BLACK BEANS, also known as *frijoles negros* or turtle beans, are a staple of Mexican, Caribbean, and Central and South American cuisines. Like all beans, they are high in soluble fiber and are a good source of fat-free protein, but they are more flavorful than most other beans.

* * *

COOKED TURKEY Use leftovers or buy precooked, diced turkey (look in the meat section of your grocery store). Or cook ground turkey, then add to the soup.

FIRST PERSON DISASTER
Go Soak Your Beans

I thought it would be great to use the beans that come in bags instead of the ones in cans—they look so authentic. I emptied the bag into the soup pot and cooked the soup according to the recipe. Imagine my surprise when I tried a spoonful and cracked a tooth because those beans were still really hard.

Later, a friend who's an experienced cook explained that the beans in the cans are already cooked and only need heating up, but the dried beans in the bags are not. She told me how to soak the dried ones overnight, then to simmer them slowly until they are tender. Now I use either dried or canned beans, depending on how much time I have. And the money I save by using dried beans just might pay for my dental bill in, oh, say, 50 years.

Geoffrey L., Avon, Connecticut

gazpacho

All the best of summer in a bowl—with no cooking! Make it zesty (spicy hot) or mild, as you wish

Serves 8-10 ❋ *Prep time: 20 minutes* ❋ *Cooking time: none* ❋ *Chilling time: 1 hour*

INGREDIENTS

- **10** tomatoes
- **2** cucumbers, seeds removed, or **2** seedless cucumbers (see next page)
- **2** red bell peppers, cored and seeded
- **1** yellow bell pepper, cored and seeded
- **2** red onions, peeled
- **6** **cloves** garlic, minced
- **⅓** **cup** white wine vinegar
- **3** **teaspoons** lime juice
- **4** **cups** Sacramento tomato juice
- **¾** **cup** chopped fresh basil
- **4** **tablespoons** olive oil
- **½** **teaspoon** Tabasco
- **1¼** **teaspoons** salt
- **2** **teaspoons** black pepper

Garnish (optional): dill sprigs

1. CUT the tomatoes, cucumbers, bell peppers, and onions into 1-inch chunks. Don't mix them together yet.

2. PLACE each vegetable *by itself* into the blender or in the bowl of a food processor fitted with a steel blade and pulse until just coarsely chopped. Be careful not to over-chop—you want some texture.

3. TRANSFER vegetables to a large bowl.

4. ADD the garlic, vinegar, lime juice, tomato juice, basil, olive oil, Tabasco, salt, and pepper to vegetables. Using a large spoon, mix well, and refrigerate for at least an hour. (The longer gazpacho sits, the more its flavors develop.)

5. LADLE the soup into bowls or mugs, and garnish with dill if desired.

WHAT IS IT AND WHERE DO I FIND IT?

SEEDLESS CUCUMBERS are also referred to as English seedless or hot-house cucumbers. They are quite long and thin and are usually sold individually wrapped. They are sweeter than traditional cucumbers and are not covered with a waxy finish (used to preserve them), so you don't have to peel them.

. . .

SACRAMENTO TOMATO JUICE: This brand of tomato juice has a tremendous amount of flavor, which will enhance the soup, so try to use it if possible. You can find it in your supermarket.

☀ NOW WHAT?! ☀

🔘 **Can I serve gazpacho warm?**
Yes. You can serve it at room temperature, but its flavors are most pronounced when it is served cold.

. . .

🔘 **What wine do you serve with it?**
Try a nice dry Sauvignon Blanc or Fumé Blanc.

45

easy zucchini soup

Wondering what to do with all that zucchini from the garden? Try this easy summer soup

Serves 4-6 ✳ *Prep time: 10 minutes* ✳ *Cooking time: 20 minutes*

INGREDIENTS

- **2 tablespoons** olive oil
- **1** large onion, chopped
- **2 cloves** garlic, minced
- **6 cups** grated zucchini
- **4 cups** low-sodium chicken broth (canned or home-made—see page 50)
- **2 teaspoons** each dried flat-leaf parsley, chives, thyme, basil, and dill or **3 tablespoons** each, fresh

Salt and black pepper to taste

Garnish (optional): low-fat yogurt or grated Parmesan cheese

1. **HEAT** the oil in a large saucepan over medium heat.

2. **ADD** the onion and garlic and **SAUTÉ** (cook over medium heat, turning the food frequently so it doesn't burn) for 3 minutes. Stir in the zucchini and cook for 5 more minutes.

3. **ADD** the chicken broth and increase the heat until the mixture **BOILS** (nickel-size bubbles will form every few seconds). Reduce the heat to low and **SIMMER** (pearl-size bubbles will form every few seconds) uncovered for 10 minutes.

4. **REMOVE** soup from the heat and let it cool for 5 to 10 minutes. Add the herbs and the salt and pepper, stirring well. Taste and add additional seasonings if needed.

5. **POUR** the cooled soup into a blender or the bowl of a food processor fitted with a steel blade. Blend the soup until it is quite smooth, return it to the saucepan, and reheat.

6. **LADLE** the soup into bowls and garnish with a dollop of low-fat yogurt or a sprinkling of grated Parmesan cheese.

How do I grate zucchini without scraping my knuckles?

While you are grating, use your fingertips to hold the zucchini. When the zucchini gets short, press it down with the flat of your palm as you drag it back and forth across the grater. (If you have a food processor, use that instead, fitted with the grating disc.)

* * *

The last time I poured something hot into my blender, the glass container cracked. What happened?

The most likely explanation is that the container was made of untempered, rather than tempered, glass. Tempered glass can withstand sudden changes in temperature; untempered glass requires that food be cooled—or added slowly to the container so that the glass can be warmed gradually—before blending.

white bean and spinach soup

This main-dish soup warms your soul on a cold winter day—you'll make it over and over again

Serves 6-8 ✳ *Prep time: 25 minutes* ✳ *Cooking time: 35 minutes*

INGREDIENTS

- **2 cans** (**15.5 ounces** each) small white beans, drained
- **3 tablespoons** olive oil
- **1 large** onion, chopped
- **¾ pound** peeled baby carrots, chopped into ½-inch bits
- **3 stalks** of celery, washed and chopped into ½-inch slices
- **6 cups** low-sodium chicken broth (canned or home-made—see page 50)
- **8 cloves** garlic, peeled and minced
- **1** bay leaf
- **1 teaspoon** dried rosemary, crumbled
- **1 teaspoon** salt, to taste
- **1 teaspoon** celery seed
- **2 teaspoons** black pepper
- **¼ teaspoon** red pepper flakes
- **2 boxes** (**10 ounces** each) chopped spinach, thawed

1. PLACE the beans in a colander and rinse with cold water. Drain them thoroughly and set them aside in a small bowl.

2. In a 6-quart soup pot, **HEAT** the oil over medium heat for 1 minute. Add chopped onion and **SAUTÉ** (stirring frequently so the onion doesn't burn) for about 5 minutes.

3. ADD the carrots and celery, and sauté for an additional 5 minutes.

4. ADD the beans, chicken broth, garlic, bay leaf, and rosemary. Reduce the heat to low and **SIMMER** (pearl-size bubbles will form every few seconds) for 20 minutes.

5. REMOVE the bay leaf (it adds wonderful flavor to food but is not enjoyable to chew).

6. ADD the salt, celery seed, black pepper, and red pepper flakes. Cook for an additional 5 minutes. Taste for seasoning; add salt or pepper as you wish.

7. REMOVE the soup from the heat and let it cool for about 5 minutes. Pour half of the soup into a blender and blend about 30 seconds, until the mixture is smooth. Return the puréed portion to the chunky soup in the pot and stir to combine.

8. STIR in the spinach. Cook for an additional minute.

9. LADLE the soup into bowls and serve.

For a hearty meal, serve soup with a green salad and warm sourdough or French bread.

chicken stock

Homemade stock, the secret that separates good soups from great ones—use it whenever a recipe calls for chicken broth

Yields 10–12 cups ✳ *Prep time: 20 minutes* ✳ *Cooking time: 3 hours*

INGREDIENTS

- **3 pounds** chicken bones, wings, necks, backs, skin (and giblets, if available)
- **2** onions, unpeeled and quartered
- **2** celery ribs, cut into 2-inch pieces
- **2** carrots, cut into 2-inch pieces
- **2** leeks, washed and chopped
- **4 cloves** garlic, unpeeled
- **1** bay leaf
- **1 sprig** fresh thyme or ¼ teaspoon dried thyme
- **5 sprigs** fresh parsley
- **10** black peppercorns or **2 teaspoons** black pepper
- Salt as desired
- **16 cups** cold water (or enough to cover ingredients)

1. PLACE all the ingredients in a large (at least 6-quart) stockpot. Bring mixture to a **boil** (nickel-size bubbles will form every few seconds) and cook for 10 minutes. You will see some dark foam forming on the surface. Skim that off with a spoon and discard.

2. REDUCE the heat and **SIMMER** (pearl-size bubbles will form every few seconds) uncovered for 2 to 3 hours, skimming foam from the top occasionally.

3. SCOOP out the chicken with a slotted spoon and discard. Allow the soup to cool slightly.

4. POUR the stock through a large, fine-mesh sieve or strainer into a large **heatproof** bowl (one that doesn't conduct heat; try one that's glass or ceramic, not metal) that you've placed in the sink. Take care not to splash yourself when pouring the hot liquid through the sieve.

5. PRESS the bones and vegetables that remain in the strainer with a spoon until all the broth is released, then discard them. Cool the stock quickly by placing it in a sink filled with cold water. This will prevent bacteria formation. Chill the stock in the refrigerator and remove any fat that rises to the surface.

How do I get rid of the fat—fast?

You can use a fat-separator cup—an inexpensive and useful cup made of plastic or glass that has a spout at the base. When you pour the stock out of this cup, the fat stays behind—it's magical! Another way is to use a heavy zip-top plastic bag. Let the stock cool, then pour it into the bag and seal it. Put the bag in the refrigerator and prop it up so that the zip-top is on top. Let stand in the refrigerator. When the fat has risen to the top (about 10 minutes), remove the bag from the refrigerator and snip off a bottom corner of the bag, draining the stock into a container and stopping before the fat reaches the opening. Discard the bag and the fat—this is a neat trick!

• • •

How do I freeze chicken stock, and how long will it keep?

You can freeze stock in freezer-proof zip-top bags—2 cups per bag. Or freeze larger amounts in airtight plastic containers. Chicken stock can be kept frozen for up to 6 months.

3 Salads

New Wave Spinach Salad (top), Vegetable Couscous Salad (middle), and Wild Rice Salad (bottom) can be eaten as either light main courses or side dishes.

classic coleslaw

This is a traditional coleslaw—if you have a food processor to do the slicing, it's incredibly quick

Serves 6-8 ✳ *Prep time: 15 minutes* ✳ *Cooking time: none*

INGREDIENTS

- ½ **head** red cabbage (about 1 pound)
- ½ **head** green or white cabbage (about 1 pound)
- 4 large carrots, peeled (or 3 cups packaged shredded carrots)

DRESSING

- 2 **cups** light mayonnaise
- ¼ **cup** Dijon mustard
- 1 **tablespoon** lime juice
- 2 **teaspoons** sugar
- 2 **tablespoons** white vinegar or red wine vinegar
- 2 **teaspoons** celery seeds
- 1 ½ **teaspoons** celery salt
- 1 ½ **teaspoons** black pepper

1. **CUT** all the cabbage into wedges and feed them into a food processor fitted with a thick slicing blade. (They can also be sliced into thin strips using a sharp kitchen knife.) Process cabbage in batches and transfer to a large bowl.

2. **SWITCH** over to the food processor's grating blade. Cut carrots into thirds and feed them in horizontally so that you end up with long shreds. (Or use that knife again.) Process in batches and mix into bowl with cabbage.

3. In a medium bowl, **WHISK** together remaining ingredients to make dressing.

4. **POUR** enough dressing over grated vegetables to coat. Serve cold or at room temperature.

greek salad

This modernized Greek salad combines romaine lettuce and peppery arugula in a light dressing

Serves 6-8 ✻ *Prep time: 15 minutes* ✻ *Cooking time: none*

INGREDIENTS

- **2 heads** romaine lettuce, washed and torn into bite-size pieces
- **2 bunches** arugula, washed and torn into bite-size pieces
- **1 ¼ cups** thinly sliced red onion
- **1 ¾ cups** crumbled feta cheese
- **16** cherry tomatoes, cut in half
- **16** pitted whole ripe olives

DRESSING

- **¾ cup** extra-virgin olive oil
- **6 tablespoons** lemon juice
- **2 teaspoons** dried oregano
- **½ teaspoon** dried parsley or **1 ½ teaspoons** chopped fresh parsley

Salt and black pepper to taste

1. In a large bowl, **MIX** together the lettuce, arugula, red onion, feta cheese, tomatoes, and olives.

2. In a small bowl, **WHISK** together olive oil, lemon juice, oregano, and parsley. Add salt and pepper to taste. Set aside.

3. **GENTLY POUR** dressing over lettuce mixture and **TOSS.** Serve immediately.

WHAT IS IT AND WHERE DO I FIND IT?

ARUGULA is a tangy, mustardy salad green that adds a nice bit of spice when combined with other greens. You can find it in the produce section of your supermarket.

* * *

FETA CHEESE, which is essential to any Greek salad, has a slightly salty tang. It is sold in bricks as well as crumbled and is available in the deli or dairy section of most supermarkets.

garlic-roasted potato salad

The perfect side dish for a barbecue or with a sandwich

Serves 6-8 ✳ *Prep time: 25 minutes* ✳ *Cooking time: 35 minutes*

INGREDIENTS

- **3 pounds** red potatoes, cut into 1-inch cubes
- **3 tablespoons** olive oil
- **1½ tablespoons** Dijon mustard
- **1 teaspoon** mustard powder
- **1 teaspoon** dried coriander
- **8 garlic cloves**, peeled and cut in half
- **1 tablespoon** dried parsley or **¼ cup** fresh flat-leaf parsley, chopped
- **1 tablespoon** dried basil or **¼ cup** fresh basil, chopped
- **⅔ cup** plain low-fat yogurt
- **¼ cup** green onions (white and green parts), thinly sliced
- **1¼ teaspoons** salt
- **1 teaspoon** black pepper

1. PREHEAT oven to 400°F.

2. COMBINE first six ingredients in a large mixing bowl. Place mixture in a shallow roasting pan and bake for 30 to 35 minutes, or until potatoes are tender, stirring every 5 minutes. Remove from oven and let cool to room temperature.

3. COMBINE parsley, basil, yogurt, green onions, salt, and pepper in a large bowl. Add potato mixture and stir gently, only to combine. Serve at room temperature.

✳ **NOW WHAT?!** ✳

How do I tell the difference between flat-leaf parsley and cilantro?

Cilantro, also referred to as fresh coriander, is a tangy green herb that resembles flat-leaf parsley or Italian parsley, hence the problem. The best way to tell them apart is to take a tiny taste. Cilantro is much stronger in taste than flat parsley, with hints of pepper and lemon.

classic green salad with vinaigrette

Serves 6 ✳ *Prep time: 10 minutes* ✳ *Cooking time: none*

INGREDIENTS

- **1** shallot, minced
- **1 tablespoon** Dijon mustard
- **½ cup** balsamic vinegar or red wine vinegar
- **½ teaspoon** salt
- **1 teaspoon** black pepper
- **1 tablespoon** lime juice
- **1 cup** and **2 tablespoons** olive oil

SALAD

- **8 cups** torn salad greens

Garnish (optional):
- **1 cup** chopped hazelnuts

1. In a small jar with a lid, **COMBINE** all vinaigrette ingredients. Shake well to mix. Vinaigrette yields 1 ½ cups.

2. **WASH** salad greens by swishing them in a large bowl of cold water. Drain in a colander and pat the leaves dry with paper towels. Better yet, use a salad spinner. Place the greens in the spinner's inner bowl and rinse them under cold running water. Place the inner bowl in the outer bowl, cover, and spin dry.

3. **TRANSFER** salad greens into a serving bowl. Shake vinaigrette to remix, then pour over the greens. Toss to mix. Garnish with hazelnuts and serve immediately.

✳ **NOW WHAT?!** ✳

How much vinaigrette should I use?

As much or as little as you want. If in doubt, use ⅛ cup (2 tablespoons) per serving.

caesar salad

An eggless version of a classic salad that is fabulous

Serves 6–8 ✳ *Prep time: 10-15 minutes* ✳ *Cooking time: 18 minutes*

INGREDIENTS

CROUTONS

¾ **teaspoon** garlic powder

½ **teaspoon** black pepper

1 **cup** grated Parmesan cheese

1 baguette (long loaf of French or Italian bread)

Olive oil, for brushing (approximately ⅓ **cup**)

for the croutons

1. **PREHEAT** oven to 400°F.

2. In a small bowl, **MIX** together the garlic powder, black pepper, and Parmesan cheese.

3. **SLICE** the baguette on the diagonal into ½-inch rounds (you'll get about 20 to 25 slices, depending on the size of the bread).

4. **PLACE** bread slices on a large baking sheet. Brush each slice with olive oil using a pastry brush or the back of a spoon. Sprinkle with the cheese mixture.

5. **BAKE** bread slices for 15 to 18 minutes or until they are brown and slightly crisp. Set aside to cool to room temperature. While croutons are cooling, prepare the dressing.

for the dressing

1. PLACE the lemon juice, garlic, and anchovy paste in a blender or the bowl of a food processor fitted with a steel blade. (Machine blending ensures a smooth consistency.) Blend or pulse until the mixture is combined.

2. ADD mustards. Blend or pulse to combine.

3. While motor is running, gradually **ADD** Parmesan cheese, oil, salt, and pepper. Blend or pulse until mixture is smooth.

for the salad

1. CUT off the base of the romaine lettuce and discard the tough outer leaves. Romaine can be very sandy—be sure to rinse whole leaves thoroughly under cool running water or in a pot of cool water. Pat dry with paper towels or use a salad spinner. Cut or tear the lettuce into bite-size pieces.

2. Place the lettuce leaves in a large serving bowl. Drizzle the dressing over the lettuce and **TOSS** gently. Garnish with the cooled croutons. Serve immediately.

DRESSING

- ½ **cup** cold lemon juice
- **5 cloves** garlic, peeled
- 1 ½-2 **teaspoons** anchovy paste
- 1 ¼ **teaspoons** Dijon mustard
- ¾ **teaspoon** dry mustard
- **6 tablespoons** Parmesan cheese, grated
- 1 **cup** plus **2 tablespoons** canola oil
- ¼ **teaspoon** salt
- 1 **teaspoon** pepper

SALAD

- **2 heads** of romaine lettuce

WHAT IS IT AND WHERE DO I FIND IT?

ANCHOVY PASTE: You can use canned or jarred anchovies in the dressing, but the tubes of paste, which have vinegar and spices mixed in, are more convenient for cooking. Look for the paste in grocery stores (near the canned anchovies) or in specialty food markets. Store opened tubes in the refrigerator.

* * *

DRY MUSTARD is powdered mustard seeds. It's available in the spice section of any supermarket.

wild rice salad

Orange juice and dried cherries complement the nutty flavor of wild rice

Serves 4–6 ✳ *Prep time: 15 minutes* ✳ *Cooking time: 40 minutes*

INGREDIENTS

- **1 cup** uncooked wild rice
- **1 ½ cups** low-sodium chicken broth
- **1 ½ cups** water
- **1 cup** pine nuts (see next page) or slivered almonds
- **1 cup** dried cherries (see next page) or dried cranberries or raisins
- **½ cup** chopped dried apricots
- **¼ cup** minced shallots
- **¼ cup** canola oil
- **⅓ cup** orange juice
- **1 tablespoon** balsamic vinegar
- **½ teaspoon** dried thyme
- **½ teaspoon** salt

1. RINSE wild rice in a strainer under cold water. (You must rinse it because it's gathered directly from marsh grasses and may contain dirt or twigs.)

2. In a large saucepan, combine rice, broth, and water. Bring to a **BOIL** over high heat so you see nickel-size bubbles forming at the surface.

3. Once it's boiling, immediately **REDUCE** heat to low and **SIMMER** (a few pearl-size bubbles will form every minute) uncovered for 40 minutes. Do not stir.

4. DRAIN rice in a colander or strainer. (Take a taste—it should be a bit crunchy.)

5. In a large bowl, **COMBINE** rice with remaining ingredients. Mix well and let stand at room temperature for up to 4 hours or until ready to serve.

WHAT IS IT AND WHERE DO I FIND IT?

PINE NUTS (also called pignoli nuts) are edible seeds that grow in the cones of various pine trees. Although expensive, they add wonderful flavor and crunch. Pine nuts are about the size of TicTacs, and they are usually sold in small containers in the nuts section of grocery, health food, and gourmet food stores. Store them in the refrigerator.

* * *

DRIED CHERRIES can be found in the produce section of most supermarkets. If you can't find them or don't like cherries, use dried cranberries. Dried fruit keeps well if stored in a plastic bag in the cupboard.

For those who love their food full of flavor and texture, take a bite of Wild Rice Salad.

warm lentil salad

Lentils aren't just for soup—try them in this salad and experience their hearty flavor

Serves 4-6 ✷ *Prep time: 15 minutes* ✷ *Cooking time: 30 minutes*

INGREDIENTS

- 4½ **cups** water
- 1¼ **cups** dried lentils (picked over, see next page)
- ¼ **cup** olive oil
- 2 **tablespoons** red wine vinegar
- 2 **tablespoons** orange juice
- 1 **teaspoon** dried oregano
- 3 **cloves** garlic, minced
- ½ **teaspoon** dried chervil or parsley
- ¼ **teaspoon** salt
- ½ **teaspoon** black pepper
- 4 **ounces** feta cheese, crumbled
- 3 **cups** torn Bibb or romaine lettuce, rinsed and dried

1. In a saucepan, **COMBINE** water and lentils over medium heat and bring to a **BOIL** (so you see nickel-size bubbles).

2. As soon as the water bubbles, **COVER** the saucepan and reduce heat to low. **SIMMER** (with pearl-size bubbles coming to the surface every minute or so) until lentils are chewable but not mushy, about 25 to 30 minutes. **DRAIN** lentils in a colander and set aside.

3. In a medium-size bowl, **COMBINE** oil, vinegar, orange juice, oregano, garlic, chervil, salt, and pepper.

4. **ADD** lentils, feta cheese, and lettuce and toss gently.

5. **SERVE** warm or at room temperature with toast points or pita bread.

WHAT IS IT AND WHERE DO I FIND IT?

LENTILS are slightly smaller and flatter than peas. There are several varieties, which are easily distinguished from one another because they are naturally different colors. The kinds found most often in supermarkets are green or brown. French lentils are greenish and very tiny—about the size of pinheads. Indian lentils are bright orange. Lentils are sold in bags in supermarkets; health food stores and Middle Eastern or Indian groceries sell them bagged or in bulk. Unlike dried beans, lentils don't need to be soaked before cooking. You should sort through them, however, discarding any stems or bits of gravel you may find, then rinse them in a colander before cooking with them.

FIRST PERSON DISASTER

Bubbles, Toil, and Trouble

It was my first time cooking lentils. I liked the fact that you didn't have to soak them like other dried beans. So I popped them in a pot with water, covered the pot, and turned the stove to low to simmer them. The meaning of the word "low" is clearly open for discussion in cooking. I turned my stove to its lowest setting. Every now and then I checked the pot. The lentils were just lying there in the water. After 25 minutes, I tasted the lentils. They were as hard as pebbles. I called my mom. What went wrong? She asked if I had seen any bubbles coming to the surface while the lentils were cooking. Well, no, not really. "Then you weren't cooking them, you were just warming them." Swell. She suggested I crank up the stove to a higher setting and let the lentils simmer. After 10 minutes, I could taste the difference. I had cooked lentils at last!

Jesse R., Yonkers, New York

new wave spinach salad

Couldn't be easier—instead of the traditional spinach salad with bacon, this one features fruit and lemon juice

Serves 6 ✳ *Prep time: 10-15 minutes* ✳ *Cooking time: none*

DRESSING

- ¼ **cup** lemon juice
- 8 **tablespoons** canola oil
- 2 **tablespoons** honey
- 1 **teaspoon** Dijon mustard
- 2 **cloves** garlic, peeled and minced
- ½ **teaspoon** salt
- 1 **teaspoon** black pepper

INGREDIENTS

- 3 **cups** torn spinach leaves, washed and dried
- 3 **cups** torn red-leaf lettuce, washed and dried
- 2 ripe kiwi fruit, peeled and thinly sliced
- 1 **can (11 ounces)** mandarin oranges, drained
- ½ **cup** dried cranberries
- 1 **cup** red onion, thinly sliced
- 6 **ounces** soft goat cheese, cut into six ½-inch-thick rounds

Bread

1. In a small bowl, **WHISK** together lemon juice, oil, honey, mustard, garlic, salt, and pepper. Set aside.

2. **COMBINE** spinach and lettuce in a large bowl.

3. **POUR** dressing over greens and toss to coat.

4. **DIVIDE** greens among 6 plates and garnish each with kiwi, mandarin oranges, cranberries, red onion, and a round of goat cheese. Serve with a crusty slice of bread.

WHAT IS IT AND WHERE DO I FIND IT?

DRIED CRANBERRIES: They are sold in small bags and can be found in the produce section of most supermarkets and health food and gourmet stores. If you can't find them, use dried cherries instead. As a last resort, you can substitute raisins.

* * *

KIWI FRUIT: Once an exotic rarity imported from New Zealand, the kiwi is now grown in the United States and is available year-round in most supermarket produce sections. Although the skin is a little hard to remove, do your best, since it's too fuzzy to eat. Use a sharp knife.

How can I tell if a kiwi is ripe?

A ripe kiwi will give slightly when you touch it and will keep at room temperature for 2 to 3 days.

* * *

I have a really hard time cutting goat cheese into rounds. Any ideas?

Yes, several. For starters, the cheese will slice more easily if you cut it while it's cold, then use it at room temperature. Cut it with a sharp knife, or use dental floss to cut through it.

New Wave Spinach Salad makes a gorgeous main course for an elegant lunch.

asparagus salad with parmesan

If it's spring, it must be asparagus season—it's perfect in salad

Serves 6 ✳ *Prep time: 10 minutes* ✳ *Cooking time: 1 minute*

INGREDIENTS

2 pounds pencil-thin asparagus, ends trimmed (see note)

DRESSING

½ **cup** olive oil

4 tablespoons champagne
vinegar or white wine
vinegar

1 ½ **tablespoons** Dijon mustard

1 tablespoon minced shallots

½ **teaspoon** black pepper

¼ **teaspoon** salt

½ **cup** grated Parmesan cheese
(see note)

1. Bring a large pot of water to a **BOIL** (you'll see nickel-size bubbles roiling up). Add the asparagus and reduce the heat to a **SIMMER** (cooking gently in water that's bubbling slightly) for 1 minute or until asparagus is just tender. Drain immediately in a colander and rinse under cold water to stop the cooking process.

2. Pat asparagus dry with paper towels and place in a serving bowl.

3. In a small bowl, **WHISK** together all dressing ingredients except Parmesan. Gently pour over asparagus and toss to coat.

4. SPRINKLE with Parmesan cheese and serve.

How do I trim asparagus?

Take hold of an asparagus stalk with both hands—one at the root end and one at the tip. Bend it until it snaps, and discard the bottom. If this strikes you as too wasteful (sometimes you'll lose half the stalk), there's nothing wrong with cutting off the tough bottom end with a knife. Pencil-thin asparagus doesn't require peeling, but if it's fatter than your little finger, peel the bottom as you would a carrot.

* * *

I always overcook my asparagus. How do I avoid that?

Ideally, asparagus should be cooked standing up in water with the tender tips above water level. Use kitchen string to tie the stalks together so that they'll stand up easily. If the asparagus is thin, it won't take more than a minute or two to cook. If it's thick, cook it a bit longer but check it frequently to avoid overcooking.

* * *

I'd like to use fresh Parmesan cheese. Is it hard to grate?

Fresh Parmesan cheese tastes so much better than the prepackaged grated kind—you won't believe it until you try it. The good news is that a chunk of fresh Parmesan cheese will last a month or two in the refrigerator. To shave it, use a vegetable (or carrot) peeler. To grate it, get out your cheese grater.

vegetable couscous salad

Couscous, a lovely cross between rice and barley, lends texture and flavor to any salad

Serves 6 ✳ *Prep time: 15 minutes* ✳ *Cooking time: 6 minutes*

INGREDIENTS

- 1 ½ **cups** low-sodium chicken broth
- 1 **cup** uncooked couscous
- ⅓ **pound** fresh asparagus, trimmed (see page 67) and cut into 1-inch pieces
- ⅓ **cup** chopped red bell pepper
- ⅓ **cup** chopped yellow bell pepper
- ⅔ **cup** cherry tomatoes, halved
- 3 scallions (both white and green parts), thinly sliced
- ¼ **cup** orange juice
- 2 **tablespoons** balsamic vinegar
- 2 **teaspoons** olive oil
- 1 ½ **teaspoons** dried oregano
- 1 ½ **teaspoons** black pepper
- 1 **teaspoon** ground cumin
- ¼ **teaspoon** salt
- 6 **cups** salad greens, rinsed and dried

1. In a medium saucepan, bring broth to a **BOIL** (so you see nickel-size bubbles). Remove saucepan from heat and stir in couscous.

2. **COVER** the saucepan and let stand for 5 minutes. Take a look—the couscous should be fully cooked. Fluff it with a fork and transfer to a large bowl. Set aside.

3. In another medium saucepan, bring one quart of water to a full boil (you'll see rolling nickel-size bubbles forming). **ADD** the asparagus to boiling water and cook for 1 minute. Drain in a colander and rinse immediately under cold water to stop the cooking process. Pat dry with paper towels.

4. **ADD** the asparagus, red and yellow bell peppers, tomatoes, and scallions to the couscous and toss gently.

5. In a small bowl, **WHISK** together orange juice, balsamic vinegar, olive oil, oregano, black pepper, cumin, and salt. Pour over couscous mixture and toss gently.

6. **COVER** and chill for up to 24 hours. Remove from refrigerator at least 30 minutes before serving.

Vegetable couscous salad makes a light, easy lunch.

7. When ready to serve, **ARRANGE** a bed of salad greens on plates and place a generous serving of the couscous salad (about 1 cup) in the center of each plate.

WHAT IS IT AND WHERE DO I FIND IT?

COUSCOUS: Think of couscous as the rice of North Africa. It's a tiny grain of semolina—the same grain that pasta flour is made from. Most U.S. supermarkets now carry an instant, packaged version in their ethnic or health food section.

Vegetables

Side dishes can often make the meal. Choose from Sesame Asparagus (top), Lemon-Dilled Carrots (middle), and Green Bean Medley (bottom).

roasted zucchini

An easy and delicious way to enjoy this plentiful summer vegetable—use fresh herbs if possible

Serves 4-6 ✳ *Prep time: 15 minutes* ✳ *Cooking time: 6 minutes*

INGREDIENTS

Vegetable oil cooking spray

- **4** medium zucchini
- **¼ cup** melted butter
- **¼ cup** olive oil
- **1 tablespoon** dried basil or **½ cup** fresh basil, minced
- **1 tablespoon** dried thyme or **½ cup** fresh thyme, minced
- **2 tablespoons** black pepper
- **⅔ cup** grated Parmesan cheese

1. PREHEAT the oven to 400° F.

2. SPRAY a large baking sheet with vegetable oil cooking spray.

3. SCRUB the zucchini, trim the ends, and slice them into 1-inch-thick rounds.

4. COMBINE the melted butter and olive oil in a small bowl and set aside.

5. PLACE the zucchini rounds on the baking sheet. Using a pastry brush (see page 11), brush both sides of the rounds lightly with the butter and oil mixture.

6. SPRINKLE herbs and pepper over the rounds, then sprinkle with grated Parmesan cheese.

7. BAKE the zucchini for 5 to 6 minutes or until they are golden brown.

◉ **How do I grate fresh Parmesan cheese?**

This aged Italian cheese is sold in wedges and can be found in most supermarket cheese sections. To grate it, simply use a box grater as you would for any other cheese. (The large holes work best.) For speedier cleanup, spray the grater with vegetable oil before grating. You can also use a food processor fitted with a grating disc to speed up preparation.

* * *

◉ **Why do you use both butter and oil to coat the zucchini?**

Each adds its own distinctive flavor to the zucchini. Also, the oil has a higher burning point than the butter does, allowing the zucchini to cook longer without browning too soon.

green bean medley

A colorful salad full of delicious flavor and texture

Serves 4-6 ✳ *Prep time: 15 minutes* ✳ *Cooking time: 10 minutes*

INGREDIENTS

- 1 ¼ **pounds** fresh green beans, stem ends trimmed
- 2 **tablespoons** canola or vegetable oil
- 1 red bell pepper, cored, seeded, and diced
- 1 yellow bell pepper, cored, seeded, and diced
- ⅓ **cup** chopped red onion
- 2 **teaspoons** minced garlic
- 1 **teaspoon** dried basil
- ½ **teaspoon** dried thyme
- ½ **teaspoon** black pepper
- ¾ **cup** grated Parmesan cheese

1. MICROWAVE the green beans in a covered microwavable dish with 1 or 2 tablespoons of water for 2 to 3 minutes or until crisp but tender. Drain them in a colander, then rinse with very cold water to stop the cooking process and drain again. Cut beans into 2-inch pieces and set aside.

2. HEAT the oil in a large, heavy skillet over medium heat for 30 seconds. **ADD** the bell peppers, onion, and garlic and cook for 2 to 3 minutes or until vegetables are slightly soft.

3. ADD the basil, thyme, and pepper and cook for 1 minute.

4. ADD the cooled green beans and cook until heated through, about 2 minutes, while stirring to combine.

5. REMOVE the vegetables from the heat and stir in ½ cup of the Parmesan cheese.

6. TRANSFER the vegetables to a serving bowl and sprinkle with remaining cheese. Serve immediately.

Green Bean Medley is a feast for both the eye and the palate.

spinach with white beans

Equally delicious served hot, cold, or at room temperature; ideal with a grilled fish fillet or chicken breast

Serves 4-6 ✳ *Prep time: 10 minutes* ✳ *Cooking time: 15-20 minutes*

INGREDIENTS

- **2-3 tablespoons** vegetable oil
- **6 cloves** garlic, minced
- **2 large** leeks (white and pale-green parts), washed, dried, and sliced thin, or 1 cup chopped onion
- **2 cans** (**14½ ounces** each) diced tomatoes, with juice
- **2 boxes** (**10 ounces** each) frozen cut leaf spinach, thawed and squeezed dry (see page 23)
- **2 cans** (**15½ ounces** each) small white beans, rinsed and drained
- **1 teaspoon** dried thyme
- **½ teaspoon** dried basil
- **½ teaspoon** dried oregano
- Salt and black pepper to taste
- **1 tablespoon** lemon juice

1. HEAT the oil in a large nonstick skillet over medium heat for 30 seconds.

2. SAUTÉ the garlic and leeks or onion (cooking over medium heat, stirring occasionally so they don't burn) for 3 to 4 minutes.

3. STIR in the tomatoes and their juices and simmer for 5 to 6 minutes.

4. ADD the spinach to the mixture and stir to combine. Continue cooking until the vegetables are heated through, about 2 to 3 minutes.

5. STIR in the beans, thyme, basil, and oregano, and cook the mixture for an additional 5 to 7 minutes. Add salt and pepper to taste and sprinkle with lemon juice.

6. TRANSFER the vegetables to a bowl and serve.

LEEKS are related to onions and have a sweet, mild, oniony flavor that works well in soups, potato dishes, and stews. (Leeks look a bit like large scallions.) You want young, tender leeks that are about 1 inch in diameter and about 9 to 12 inches long. Their stalks can be full of dirt and so must be thoroughly washed. To clean them, trim off the rough ends of the dark green leaves and discard. Make a slit down the center of the leek and pull it apart. Wash each half thoroughly under cold water, bending the layers back to rinse away every bit of grit that's hidden between them. Pat dry with paper towels.

sesame asparagus

When asparagus is not available, you can substitute broccoli—either one is a wonderful accompaniment to grilled entrées, from shrimp to steak

Serves 6 ✳ *Prep time: 10-15 minutes* ✳ *Cooking time: 8-10 minutes*

INGREDIENTS

- **2 pounds** fresh asparagus, ends trimmed (see page 67) and stalks cut into thirds
- **2 tablespoons** vegetable oil
- **4 teaspoons** garlic, minced
- **2-4 tablespoons** sesame oil
- **1½ tablespoons** lemon juice
- **2 teaspoons** low-sodium soy sauce

Salt and pepper to taste

- **3 tablespoons** sesame seeds

1. BRING a medium-size pot of water to a boil over high heat (you'll see nickel-size bubbles). Drop in the asparagus, reduce the heat to medium, and cook for about 1 minute, until it is crisp but tender.

2. DRAIN the asparagus in a colander and immediately rinse under cold water to stop the cooking process. Drain again and set aside.

3. HEAT the vegetable oil in a large nonstick skillet over medium-high heat for 1 minute.

4. ADD the garlic and cook, stirring continually for about 30 seconds. (Be careful not to let the garlic burn.)

5. ADD the asparagus and 2 tablespoons of sesame oil to the skillet, stirring constantly to coat the asparagus with oil. (Add additional sesame oil if needed.) Cook the asparagus, tossing, for 1 to 2 additional minutes.

6. POUR the lemon juice and soy sauce over the asparagus and stir well. Add salt and pepper to taste. Sprinkle sesame seeds over the asparagus and toss well.

7. TRANSFER the asparagus to a dish and serve.

Sesame seeds plus a bit of soy sauce and lemon juice turn ordinary asparagus into an exciting side dish.

zucchini squares

Serve these delicious creations as a side dish or as a main course for brunch or lunch

Serves 6 as a side dish; serves 4 as a main course ❋ *Prep time: 25 minutes*
❋ *Cooking time: 20-25 minutes*

INGREDIENTS

Vegetable oil cooking spray

- **3 pounds** zucchini, scrubbed clean, trimmed, and grated (see page 47)
- **2 tablespoons** butter
- **2 tablespoons** vegetable oil
- **5 cloves** garlic, chopped
- **1 cup** chopped scallions (white and green parts)
- **1 large egg**, lightly beaten
- **2 large eggs**, whites only, lightly beaten
- ½ **cup** grated Parmesan cheese
- ⅓ **cup** bread crumbs
- 1 ½ **tablespoons** dried basil or 1 ¼ **cup** fresh basil, rinsed and chopped

Salt and pepper to taste

1. PREHEAT the oven to 350°F.

2. COAT an 8-inch-square baking pan with vegetable oil cooking spray and set aside.

3. SPREAD the grated zucchini on paper towels or clean dish towels, rolling them up jelly-roll style to absorb any excess water. Place the zucchini in a large bowl and set aside.

4. HEAT the butter and oil in a large skillet over medium-high heat until butter melts (about 30 seconds).

5. ADD the garlic and scallions to the skillet and cook over medium heat, stirring frequently, until lightly browned, about 2 to 3 minutes.

6. ADD the scallion mixture to the zucchini, stirring to combine. Add the whole egg, egg whites, Parmesan cheese, bread crumbs, basil, and salt and pepper to taste. Stir to combine.

7. TRANSFER the zucchini mixture to the baking dish and bake 20 to 25 minutes until firm in the center and light brown on top. To test that it's firm in the center, jiggle the pan; if the center still quivers, bake the zucchini for another 2 to 3 minutes.

8. CUT the zucchini into squares and serve immediately.

FIRST PERSON DISASTER

"Runny" Late

My guests were coming for brunch at 11:30 a.m. and I was running late. I had grated the zucchini for a zucchini quiche and had left them in paper towels to soak up all the liquid. I had put out a wonderful bread I had bought at the farmer's market and a salad. Just as I was setting the table, my guests rang the bell. I poured them each a glass of wine and headed back in to throw the quiche ingredients together—now I was 10 more minutes behind. As I poured the zucchini mixture into the baking dish, I had the bright idea of turning up the heat to speed along the baking. So instead of baking the quiche at 350°F for 40 minutes, I turned up the oven to 450°F and baked it for 20 minutes. The result? Burnt on top, dried-out at the edges, and runny in the middle. By trying to save 20 minutes, I ruined my brunch. At least the salad and bread were edible.

Marjorie P., Riverhead, Connecticut

acorn squash with herbed citrus sauce

Serve alongside any pork or poultry dish

Serves 6 ✳ *Prep time: 10 minutes* ✳ *Cooking time: 1 hour*

INGREDIENTS

- **3** medium acorn squash, halved and seeded
- Salt and black pepper to taste
- **3 tablespoons** butter
- **4 teaspoons** dark brown sugar, packed
- **½ cup** orange juice
- **1 tablespoon** orange zest (see next page)
- **1 tablespoon** lemon zest (see next page)
- **1 teaspoon** dried thyme
- **1 teaspoon** dried oregano
- **1 teaspoon** ground cinnamon

1. PREHEAT oven to 350° F.

2. SEASON the squash with salt and pepper to taste. Place squash halves in a baking pan, cut side down, and add 1 inch of water to the pan.

3. BAKE the squash, uncovered, 50 to 60 minutes or until the fleshy underside is tender when pierced with a fork. Remove the squash halves from the oven and invert them so that the flesh side is up. Set them aside.

4. COMBINE the butter, brown sugar, orange juice, orange zest, lemon zest, thyme, and oregano in a small saucepan. Cook over medium-low heat for 5 minutes, stirring constantly, until the sauce has the consistency of a vinaigrette salad dressing.

5. SPOON the sauce evenly into the scooped-out squash halves, stirring slightly to blend. Return the squash to the oven and bake for 5 to 10 minutes.

6. REMOVE the squash halves from the oven. Sprinkle with cinnamon and serve immediately.

WHAT IS IT AND WHERE DO I FIND IT?

ACORN SQUASH is about the size of a large grapefruit. It has thick, dark green skin, with deep grooves running up and down its sides. Inside, the flesh is yellow-orange (it's loaded with vitamin A). It's available in produce sections most frequently during fall and winter.

● ● ●

LEMON, LIME, AND ORANGE ZESTS are not sold in stores—you have to make zest yourself. How? Get a fresh lemon, lime, or orange, a cheese grater, and a plate. Wash the fruit. Put the plate under the grater and rub the fruit on the side of the grater with the smallest holes. You'll see little powdery flecks on the plate—that's the zest. (Avoid grating the white pith under the brightly colored skin—it's not at all tasty.)

lemon-dilled carrots

Lemon and dill add a sophisticated touch to a tried-and-true favorite

Serves 6-8 ✳ *Prep time: 10 minutes* ✳ *Cooking time: 10 minutes*

INGREDIENTS

- **10** medium-size carrots, peeled and sliced on the diagonal
- **1 ½ teaspoons** cornstarch
- **1 tablespoon** plus **1 teaspoon** lemon juice
- **½ cup** water
- **1 ¼ teaspoons** margarine
- **1 teaspoon** dried dill or **2 teaspoons** chopped fresh dill
- **½ teaspoon** grated lemon zest (see page 83)
- **¼ teaspoon** salt
- **1 teaspoon** black pepper
- **2 teaspoons** honey
- **Garnish** (optional): fresh dill sprigs

1. STEAM the sliced carrots in a vegetable steamer for 2 minutes or until they are crisp but tender (see note on next page on how to use a steamer). Or place the carrots in a microwavable dish with ½ cup of water and microwave on high for 3 to 4 minutes. Drain the carrots in a colander (but don't run cold water over them after steaming). Set the colander aside and cover it with a tent made from aluminum foil to keep carrots warm.

2. COMBINE the cornstarch and lemon juice in a small saucepan, stirring until they are blended. Then stir in the water.

3. PLACE the pan over medium heat and cook, stirring constantly, until the mixture thickens. It should look like very thin pancake batter.

4. ADD the margarine, dill, lemon zest, salt, pepper, and honey. Cook, stirring the sauce constantly, until the margarine melts.

5. TRANSFER the carrots to a serving dish and pour the sauce over them, tossing to combine. Garnish if desired and serve.

Lemon and dill turn everyday carrots into a gourmet side dish.

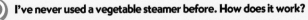

✳ NOW WHAT?! ✳

I've never used a vegetable steamer before. How does it work?

A steamer is a perforated metal basket that stands above the water level in a saucepan (see page 7 for illustration). Place the steamer in a pot with a lid. (The lid should fit snugly so that steam doesn't escape—this would defeat the purpose.) Pour water in the pot to just below the bottom of the steamer. Place the food in the steamer, cover the pot, and cook for as long as the recipe stipulates. When the food is ready, use an oven mitt to slowly remove the lid.

roasted red potatoes

The perfect accompaniment to so many entrées—and best of all, they are so easy to prepare

Serves 8 ✳ *Prep time: 10 minutes* ✳ *Cooking time: 35-40 minutes*

INGREDIENTS

3 pounds small red-skinned potatoes, cut into 1½-inch pieces

2 tablespoons chopped garlic

1½ tablespoons dried rosemary, crumbled, or **3 tablespoons** fresh rosemary, minced

1 teaspoon salt

1 teaspoon black pepper

⅓ cup olive oil

1. **PREHEAT** oven to 400°F.

2. **COMBINE** all of the ingredients in a large bowl. Toss so that potatoes are coated on all sides with the oil and seasonings.

3. **TRANSFER** potatoes to a large baking dish or roasting pan. Bake for 35 to 40 minutes or until potatoes are tender inside and browned and crisp outside. Stir potatoes every 15 minutes so that they cook evenly.

4. **SERVE** immediately.

garlic-mashed potatoes

A new spin on an old-time standard

Serves 6-8 ✳ *Prep time: 15 minutes* ✳ *Roasting time for garlic: 45 minutes* ✳ *Cooking time for potatoes: 15–20 minutes*

INGREDIENTS

- **1** large whole head of garlic
- **1½ tablespoons** olive oil
- **2 pounds** Yukon gold potatoes, peeled and quartered
- **½ cup** skim milk
- **¾ cup** plain low-fat yogurt
- **1 teaspoon** salt
- **1 teaspoon** black pepper

1. PREHEAT oven to 375°F.

2. REMOVE papery skin from garlic head, keeping it whole. Rub oil over garlic head and wrap in foil. Bake for 45 minutes, then cool for 10 minutes. Separate the cloves and squeeze to extract the pulp. Discard skins and set garlic aside.

3. PLACE potatoes in a large pot and cover with salted water. Bring to a boil on medium-high heat and cook for 15 to 20 minutes or until they are tender when pierced with a fork. Drain in a colander and set aside.

4. HEAT milk in a small saucepan over low heat until just warm, or microwave in a microwave dish for 30 seconds.

5. PLACE cooked potatoes in a medium-size mixing bowl. Pour milk over potatoes and, using an electric mixer, **BEAT** at medium speed until potatoes are smooth. Beat in yogurt, salt, and pepper; mix until smooth. Add garlic pulp and stir with a spoon to combine. Season with additional salt and pepper to suit your taste.

6. SERVE immediately.

sweet potato gratin

Gratin is a dish topped with cheese or bread crumbs—here it's Parmesan cheese and chives

Serves 6-8 ✳ *Prep time: 20 minutes* ✳ *Cooking time: 1 hour 15 minutes*

INGREDIENTS

Vegetable oil or cooking oil spray

- ¾ **cup** light cream
- ¾ **cup** sherry or white wine
- 2 **teaspoons** minced shallots
- ½ **teaspoon** salt
- 1 **teaspoon** ground white pepper (see next page)
- ½ **teaspoon** ground nutmeg
- 1 ½ **pounds** white potatoes
- 1 ½ **pounds** sweet potatoes
- 2 **teaspoons** dried chives, or ¼ **cup** chopped fresh chives
- 1 **cup** grated Parmesan cheese

1. PREHEAT oven to 375°F.

2. COAT a 9-inch-square baking pan with vegetable oil or cooking oil spray.

3. COMBINE cream, sherry, shallots, salt, white pepper, and nutmeg in a small bowl and set aside.

4. FILL two large bowls three-quarters full of cold water. **PEEL** the white potatoes and slice them into ¼-inch rounds. Drop the slices into one of the bowls so they don't discolor. Peel and slice the sweet potatoes and place them in the other bowl.

5. DRAIN the potatoes and pat dry. Using about half the slices, **ARRANGE** a single layer of white potatoes on the bottom of the pan; overlap the slices slightly. Drizzle with ¼ of the cream mixture.

6. COVER the layer of white potatoes with a layer of sweet potatoes, overlapping the slices. (Again, use about half the slices.) Drizzle lightly with $1/4$ of the cream mixture. Sprinkle half of the chives and half of the Parmesan cheese over this layer.

7. LAYER the remaining white potatoes on top of the cheese and chives. Drizzle with $1/4$ of the cream mixture. Add a layer of the remaining sweet potatoes. Pour the rest of the cream mixture over the potatoes. Sprinkle with the remaining chives and Parmesan cheese.

8. COVER the pan with aluminum foil and bake for 35 minutes. Remove the foil and bake for 40 minutes or until the cheese is browned and the potatoes are tender. Serve hot.

WHAT IS IT AND WHERE DO I FIND IT?

WHITE PEPPER is made from white, rather than black, peppercorns. Because it is white, it is not visible in white cream sauces or mashed potatoes. You can find it in the spice section of your supermarket.

One-Pot Meals

Hearty, delicious meals in one dish—what could be better? Try Penne with Shrimp and Feta (top), Spinach Pie (middle), and Shepherd's Pie (bottom).

black bean chili

Black beans and ground turkey go together beautifully to create a substantially lighter chili

Serves 6-8 ✻ *Prep time: 30 minutes* ✻ *Cooking time: 50-60 minutes*

INGREDIENTS

- **1 tablespoon** olive oil
- **1** large yellow onion, chopped
- **6 cloves** garlic, minced
- **1 ¼ pounds** ground turkey
- **6 cups** canned diced tomatoes, with juices
- **2** celery ribs, washed and cut into 1-inch chunks
- **1 ½ teaspoons** Dijon mustard
- **1 ½ teaspoons** ground cumin
- **2 teaspoons** chili powder
- **4 cans** (15.5 ounces each) black beans, rinsed and drained
- **1 cup** low-sodium chicken broth
- **2 tablespoons** balsamic vinegar
- Salt and black pepper to taste
- **⅓ cup** lime juice
- **Garnish** (optional): sour cream, chopped scallions or cilantro, grated cheddar or Parmesan cheese

1. **HEAT** the oil in a large stockpot (see page 7) over medium heat for about 20 seconds.

2. **ADD** the onion and garlic and cook for 2 to 3 minutes, until the onion is translucent.

3. **ADD** the turkey, tomatoes, celery, mustard, cumin, and chili powder and cook for about 5 minutes. Break up the turkey with a long wooden spoon and stir mixture occasionally.

4. **ADD** the beans and reduce heat to low. Cook uncovered for about 40 to 45 minutes, until the soup thickens. If it thickens after 30 minutes of cooking, add some chicken broth, ¼ cup at a time.

5. **ADD** the vinegar, salt, and pepper and cook for 5 minutes. Stir in the lime juice.

6. **SERVE** garnished with sour cream, chopped scallions or cilantro, grated cheddar or Parmesan cheese, if desired.

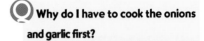
Why do I have to cook the onions and garlic first?

Sautéing onions and garlic before adding them to a soup or stew enhances the finished dish by releasing more of their flavor.

FIRST PERSON DISASTER

Burned Once, Burned Twice

It was Superbowl Sunday, a day when I always make chili for my friends. I put it all together, let it simmer on the stove and went to watch the game. What can I say? My team was ahead by one field goal, and I was screaming so loudly that I didn't hear the kitchen timer. When I finally went back to the kitchen to get more beer, I realized that the chili had been cooking for more than an hour without being stirred. And what was that horrible smell? I checked the pot and discovered that the chili had burned and stuck to the bottom of the pot.

No problem, I'll just stir the burned part in and no one will notice. Wrong! Everyone noticed. Maybe it was the mouthfuls of burned beans that gave it away. My girlfriend said I should not have stirred the burned part into the chili—if I had just poured the chili into another pot, the burned stuff would have stayed behind. Well, at least my team won. Next year it's pizza.

Michael T., Sunapee, New Hampshire

spinach pie

All the taste of spanakopita, but without the hassle of phyllo dough—flaky premade puff pastry does the job

Serves 6-8 ✳ *Prep time: 20 minutes* ✳ *Cooking time: 1 hour 15 minutes*

INGREDIENTS

- 2½ **tablespoons** olive oil
- 2½ **cups** chopped Spanish or yellow onions
- 2 **teaspoons** salt
- 2 **teaspoons** black pepper
- 3 **boxes** (**10 ounces** each) frozen chopped spinach, thawed, squeezed dry (see page 23)
- 4 extra-large whole eggs, lightly beaten
- 2 extra-large egg whites, lightly beaten
- 2½ **teaspoons** ground nutmeg
- 2 **teaspoons** dried dill or **2 tablespoons** chopped fresh dill
- ½ **cup** grated Parmesan cheese
- ⅔ **pound** feta cheese, crumbled
- ⅔ **cup** pine nuts (see page 61)
- 1 **sheet** frozen puff pastry, thawed

1. PREHEAT the oven to 375° F.

2. In a skillet, heat the olive oil over medium-high heat for 1 minute. **ADD** the onions and cook for 10 to 12 minutes, stirring frequently, so the onions don't burn. The onions should be translucent and slightly browned.

3. ADD the salt and pepper and remove the skillet from the heat. Set aside and let cool.

4. PLACE the spinach in a large bowl. Stir in the cooked onion, then the eggs, egg whites, nutmeg, dill, Parmesan cheese, feta cheese, and pine nuts.

5. ROLL out the thawed puff pastry to a ⅛-inch thickness and line a 9-inch pie plate (glass or aluminum) with it. Using a fork, crimp the edges of the pastry along the rim of the pie plate.

6. POUR the spinach mixture into the pie plate and spread it to the edges of the pan.

7. BAKE the pie for 50 to 60 minutes until the filling is set.

8. REMOVE the pie from the oven and allow it to cool to room temperature. Cut into wedges and serve.

WHAT IS IT AND WHERE DO I FIND IT?

PUFF PASTRY looks like pie dough, but it's flakier and lighter—and puffs up when cooked. Look for it in the freezer section of your supermarket. If you can't find it, use a frozen pie crust that comes in its own aluminum pie pan.

chicken pot pie

A great way to use leftover chicken or turkey—sure to warm you up on the coldest winter day

Serves 6 ✳ *Prep time: 30 minutes* ✳ *Cooking time: 55 minutes*

INGREDIENTS

- 1½ **tablespoons** olive oil
- 2 large leeks (white and pale-green parts), rinsed (see page 77) and thinly sliced
- 2¼ **cups** low-sodium chicken stock (canned or home-made—see page 50)
- 3 carrots, peeled and diced
- 8 **ounces** (about 1½ **cups**) sugar snap peas cut into 1-inch pieces, or green peas
- 1½ **cups** frozen corn kernels, thawed
- 1½ **tablespoons** dried parsley
- 1½ **teaspoons** dried thyme
- 1 **teaspoon** each salt and pepper
- 2 **tablespoons** cornstarch
- 2 **cups** cooked chicken or turkey, cut into chunks
- 1 **sheet** frozen puff pastry, thawed

(continued on next page)

1. PREHEAT oven to 475° F.

2. HEAT the oil in a skillet over medium-high heat for 1 minute. **ADD** the leeks and cook for 5 minutes, stirring occasionally. **ADD** 2 cups of stock to the skillet.

3. ADD the carrots, snap peas, corn, parsley, thyme, and salt and pepper to the skillet. Cover and simmer over low heat for 8 to 10 minutes or until the vegetables are almost tender. Uncover and cook an additional 2 to 3 minutes.

4. In a small bowl, **STIR** the cornstarch and the remaining stock together until combined. The mixture should look like a thin paste. Add it to the vegetable mixture and stir for 1 minute, until the liquid begins to thicken slightly.

5. ADD the chicken chunks to the skillet. Stir until the chicken chunks are coated.

6. TRANSFER the chicken mixture to a 2½-quart casserole dish. (The dish should have sides 3 inches high.) **PLACE** the thawed puff pastry sheet over the chicken so that it overlaps the edges of the dish slightly. **PRESS** the pastry firmly around the outside edges of the dish to seal it. **TRIM** any excess with a sharp knife and discard it. Using a sharp knife or a fork, poke several holes in the pastry.

7. Optional: **WHISK** together the egg white and the water and brush the mixture over the top of the pastry. It will give the pastry a glossy sheen.

8. BAKE the pie for 25 minutes, or until the crust is lightly browned. Serve.

(continued from previous page)
Optional:

1   egg white

1   **tablespoon** water

❋ NOW WHAT?! ❋

Q What does cornstarch do?
Cornstarch is starch that is extracted from corn kernels and reduced to a silky white powder. It acts as a thickener, especially for sauces. You must mix it with a little cool water or other liquid before adding it to a mixture or you'll get lumps in your sauce. Cornstarch is available at the supermarket.

* * *

Q I must have cooked the broth too long because it boiled away and now I don't have enough for the recipe. What do I do?
Open another can of chicken broth and make up the difference.

shepherd's pie

This traditional English pie takes a bit of time—but it's worth it!

Serves 6 ✳ *Prep time: 45 minutes* ✳ *Cooking time: 45 minutes (25 minutes for the pie, 20 minutes for the potato topping)*

INGREDIENTS

- **2 pounds** ground lamb or beef
- **1** large yellow onion, chopped
- **2-3 cloves** garlic, minced
- **2** carrots, diced
- **1** small fennel bulb, diced (see next page)
- **1** large parsnip, peeled and diced (see next page)
- **1 teaspoon** dried rosemary
- **1 teaspoon** turmeric
- **½ teaspoon** ground cinnamon
- **1 ½ cups** low-sodium canned beef broth
- **1 tablespoon** cornstarch
- **1 tablespoon** water

Salt and black pepper, to taste

for the filling

1. COOK the lamb or beef in a large skillet over medium heat for 10 to 12 minutes, until it is just done, breaking up the meat with the back of a wooden spoon. Pour the drippings into an empty can and discard them.

2. ADD the onion, garlic, carrots, fennel, parsnip, rosemary, turmeric, and cinnamon. Stir together and cook 5 minutes.

3. ADD the beef broth to the skillet and cover. Simmer over low heat for 12 to 15 minutes (pearl-size bubbles will form every few seconds). Uncover the skillet and simmer for another 2 minutes, until most of the juices have evaporated.

4. In a small bowl, **MIX** the cornstarch and water and pour the mixture into the skillet, stirring to combine it with the sauce. The sauce should thicken slightly. Season it to taste with the salt and pepper.

5. TRANSFER the mixture to a 2½-quart casserole or a baking dish with sides at least 2 inches high.

for the potato topping

1. PREHEAT the oven to 400° F.

2. BOIL the potatoes in a large pot of water for about 20 minutes or until they are just tender.

3. While the potatoes are cooking, **MELT** the butter in a small skillet over medium heat, watching it carefully so that it doesn't burn. Add the garlic and cook for about 1 minute, until it is just golden.

4. DRAIN the potatoes and transfer them to a large bowl. Add the butter and garlic mixture, plus the yogurt, milk, and Worcestershire sauce (optional).

5. BEAT the potatoes with a handheld electric mixer until they are smooth and creamy. Season them to taste with salt and pepper.

6. SPOON the potatoes over the top of the meat mixture, spreading them to the edge of the casserole.

7. BAKE the pie for 20 to 25 minutes, until the filling is heated through and the potatoes are golden brown. Cut into wedges and serve immediately.

TOPPING

- **2 pounds** white potatoes, peeled and chopped into 2-inch pieces
- **3 tablespoons** butter
- **3 tablespoons** garlic, minced
- ½ **cup** plain nonfat yogurt
- ¼ **cup** skim milk
- ½ **teaspoon** Worcestershire sauce (optional)

Salt and white pepper to taste

✳ NOW WHAT?! ✳

Can I use instant potatoes instead?
Yes. You'll need to make about 5 cups.

WHAT IS IT AND WHERE DO I FIND IT?

FENNEL is a vegetable that looks a bit like celery and is as crunchy but has a delicate feathery top. It has a spicy flavor similar to that of licorice but much more subtle. It's available at most supermarkets.

* * *

PARSNIPS are shaped like carrots but are creamy white or tan colored. They have a tough, fibrous exterior that has to be removed with a vegetable peeler. Look for parsnips in the produce section of your supermarket.

spinach lasagna

This is a crowd-pleasing make-ahead meal

Serves 6 ✳ *Prep time: 25 minutes* ✳ *Cooking time: 50 minutes*

INGREDIENTS

- 1 **tablespoon** olive oil
- 2½ **cups** button mushrooms, sliced
- 1 **cup** shredded carrots
- 1 large yellow onion, chopped
- 4 **cloves** garlic, minced
- 1 **teaspoon** dried thyme
- 5 **cups** prepared tomato sauce
- 2 **boxes** (**10 ounces** each) frozen chopped spinach, thawed, drained, and squeezed dry
- 3 **ounces** low-fat cream cheese, softened
- 1½ **cups** low-fat cottage cheese
- 1 **cup** low-fat ricotta cheese
- 2 **teaspoons** lemon juice
- 12 oven-ready lasagna noodles
- 1 **bag** (**8 ounces**) shredded part-skim mozzarella cheese
- 1 **cup** grated Parmesan cheese

1. HEAT the olive oil in a large nonstick skillet over medium-high heat for about 20 seconds, until it is hot.

2. ADD the mushrooms, carrots, onion, and garlic and **COOK** over medium heat, stirring frequently, for 3 minutes. Stir in the thyme. Remove the skillet from the heat and stir in 4 cups of the tomato sauce, reserving one cup. Set skillet aside.

3. In a medium-size bowl, **COMBINE** the spinach, cream cheese, cottage cheese, ricotta, and lemon juice. Stir the spinach-cheese mixture well and set it aside.

4. PREHEAT the oven to 325° F.

5. POUR 1 cup of the sauce into a 13 x 9-inch baking dish. Arrange 4 of the oven-ready lasagna noodles in the bottom of the baking dish.

6. SPOON ⅓ of the spinach-cream mixture over the noodles; spoon ⅓ of the mushroom-tomato mixture over the spinach; spoon ⅓ of the mozzarella cheese over the tomato mixture; sprinkle ⅓ cup of Parmesan cheese on top.

7. REPEAT the layers outlined in steps 5 and 6 twice. (Lasagna may be prepared up to this point, covered, and refrigerated for one day before baking.)

8. BAKE the lasagna uncovered for 50 minutes, until it is heated through. Serve immediately.

✳ NOW WHAT?! ✳

How will I know when the oil is hot enough to cook garlic, onions, or shallots?

The surface of the oil will shimmer slightly, but not to the point of smoking. If you are in doubt, put a drop of water or a bit of the vegetable in the oil. If it sizzles, the oil is hot enough.

• • •

How do I clean mushrooms?

Never immerse mushrooms in water, since they act like sponges and absorb liquid very quickly. The best way to clean them is to use a mushroom brush, which you can purchase at most grocery stores or any kitchen supply store. Or you can brush them off with a damp paper towel. If the mushrooms have a lot of debris on them, place them in a colander and rinse them quickly under cold water. Immediately pat them dry with paper towels.

WHAT IS IT AND WHERE DO I FIND IT?

BUTTON MUSHROOMS, tender mushrooms the size of large buttons, can be found in the produce section of most supermarkets. They also come in cans, but much of their delicate flavor is lost in the canning process, so it is important to use fresh ones to get the fullest flavor.

beef and noodle bake

Hearty food to feed a hungry crowd

Serves 8 ✻ *Prep time: 30 minutes* ✻ *Cooking time: 1 hour (can be prepared 8 hours in advance, refrigerated, then baked)*

INGREDIENTS

Vegetable oil or cooking oil spray

- **8 ounces** medium egg noodles
- **1 ½ pounds** lean ground beef
- **1 cup** sliced mushrooms
- **1 cup** chopped onion
- **3 cloves** garlic, minced
- **16 ounces** no-salt canned tomato sauce
- **1 can (14.5 ounces)** diced tomatoes, drained
- **1 teaspoon** Italian seasoning (see next page)
- **1 teaspoon** salt
- **1 teaspoon** black pepper
- **1 container (16 ounces)** nonfat cottage cheese
- **1 container (8 ounces)** fat-free sour cream
- **4 tablespoons** grated Parmesan cheese

(continued on next page)

1. PREHEAT the oven to 350° F. Coat a casserole dish with vegetable oil or cooking oil spray. Set aside.

2. COOK the noodles according to package directions. Drain them and set aside.

3. PLACE the ground beef, mushrooms, onion, and garlic in a large nonstick skillet over medium-high heat. Cook, stirring frequently, for about 6 minutes, until the beef is browned.

4. SCOOP the cooked ingredients onto a plate covered with a double layer of paper towels to absorb excess oil. Pour the oil from the skillet into an empty can and discard it. Return the cooked ingredients to the skillet.

5. ADD the tomato sauce, tomatoes, Italian seasoning, salt, and pepper and stir to combine. Cook over medium-low heat for about 12 minutes. Remove the sauce from the heat.

6. In a large bowl, **COMBINE** the cottage cheese, sour cream, and Parmesan cheese.

7. ADD the meat mixture to the bowl, together with the noodles and half of the cheese mixture. Stir to combine the ingredients.

8. SPOON the mixture into the casserole dish. (The dish can be prepared up to this point, covered with plastic wrap, and refrigerated for up to 8 hours. When ready to bake, remove the casserole from the refrigerator and let it stand at room temperature for 20 minutes before baking.)

9. BAKE uncovered for 25 minutes. Remove the dish from the oven and sprinkle the top with the shredded cheese. Return the dish to the oven for an additional 5 minutes or until the cheese has melted. Serve.

WHAT IS IT AND WHERE DO I FIND IT?

ITALIAN SEASONING can be found in most supermarket spice sections, or you can use a combination of thyme, oregano, basil, and marjoram.

(continued from previous page)

4 ounces shredded low-fat sharp cheddar or Monterey Jack cheese, or a combination

✳ NOW WHAT?! ✳

Can I substitute fresh herbs for dried ones and vice versa?

Yes, although fresh herbs have brighter flavors than dried herbs. One tablespoon of a chopped fresh herb is the equivalent of 1 teaspoon of a dried herb. The ratio is 3 fresh herbs to 1 dried herb.

• • •

What should I do if my dried herbs are more than six months old and have lost some of their flavor?

Add a bit more of the dried herb to the recipe to increase the flavor. (It's best to replace dried herbs after six months.)

deep-dish beef burgundy pie

A classic dish that is sure to please

Serves 6 ✳ *Prep time: 45 minutes* ✳ *Cooking time: 45 minutes (20 minutes for the filling, 25 minutes for the pie)*

INGREDIENTS

- **1 tablespoon** flour
- **½ teaspoon** each salt and black pepper
- **2 pounds** boneless beef chuck, cut into 1½-inch pieces
- **1 tablespoon** olive oil
- **3 tablespoons** butter
- **2** onions, peeled and diced
- **2 teaspoons** minced garlic
- **2 cups** diced carrots
- **2 cups** diced red potatoes
- **1½ tablespoons** Dijon mustard
- **1 cup** red wine
- **1 cup** canned beef broth
- **1 tablespoon** balsamic vinegar
- **2 tablespoons** dried parsley

(continued on next page)

1. COMBINE the flour, salt, and pepper in a large bowl. **ADD** the beef and toss with a fork until the pieces are thoroughly coated with the flour mixture. Set the bowl aside.

2. HEAT the olive oil and 2 tablespoons of the butter in a large skillet over medium heat until the butter melts. Add the onions and garlic and cook for 2 to 3 minutes. Transfer the vegetables from the pan to a plate, using a slotted spoon. Set the plate aside.

3. ADD the beef to the same skillet and cook for 2 to 3 minutes on each side, until the pieces are brown. (The browning may have to be finished in batches.)

4. ADD the cooked onions and garlic, plus the carrots, potatoes, mustard, red wine, broth, vinegar, parsley, thyme, and brown sugar to the skillet and stir to combine. Increase the heat to high and bring the mixture to a boil. Reduce the heat to medium-low and **SIMMER** (a few pearl-size bubbles will appear every minute) uncovered for 1 hour.

5. When the beef is almost done simmering, melt the remaining butter in a medium-size skillet over low heat.

Add the mushrooms, increase the heat to medium-high, and cook, stirring frequently, for 2 minutes.

6. **ADD** the mushrooms and peas to the beef mixture. Continue simmering for 3 minutes.

7. **PREHEAT** the oven to 425° F.

8. **POUR** the beef mixture into a 2½-quart casserole dish. Place the puff pastry sheet on top. Trim the edges, leaving a 1-inch overhang. **CRIMP** (pinch in a pretty pattern) the pastry to seal the edge of the dish. Place the dish on a baking sheet. **VENT** the pastry by cutting a few slits in the top. (Venting lets steam release slowly from the pie so that the filling does not boil over.)

9. **BAKE** the pie for 25 minutes or until the pastry is lightly browned. Serve immediately.

(continued from previous page)

- 2 **teaspoons** dried thyme
- 2 **tablespoons** brown sugar
- ½ **pound** fresh mushrooms, sliced
- 1 **cup** frozen green peas, thawed
- 1 **sheet** frozen puff pastry, thawed and rolled to ¼-inch thickness (see page 95)

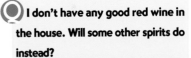

✳ **NOW WHAT?!** ✳

🔵 **I don't have any good red wine in the house. Will some other spirits do instead?**

Yes, you can substitute sherry or Madeira—use the same amount the recipe calls for. Otherwise, borrow some good red wine from a neighbor. The wine or spirits you use will impact the flavor of the dish.

chicken and wild rice casserole

Turn chicken into a one-dish wonder with this delicious combination of wild rice and mushrooms

Serves 6 ✳ *Prep time: 25 minutes (not including cooking time for wild rice)*
✳ *Cooking time: 50 minutes*

INGREDIENTS

- **2 packages (6 ounces** each) wild rice, cooked according to package instructions
- ½ **teaspoon** salt
- **1 teaspoon** black pepper
- ½ **teaspoon** paprika
- **1 teaspoon** garlic powder
- **1 tablespoon** butter
- **1 teaspoon** canola oil
- **6** skinless, boneless chicken breast halves
- **2** medium shallots, minced
- **3 cups** sliced mushrooms
- 2½ **cups** low-sodium chicken stock (canned or home-made—see page 50)
- ⅔ **cup** dry sherry (see next page)
- **1 tablespoon** cornstarch
- **3 tablespoons** water
- **1 teaspoon** dried rosemary, crumbled

1. PREHEAT the oven to 375° F.

2. COOK the wild rice according to the package directions. Spoon the rice into an ungreased 9 x 13-inch baking dish and set it aside.

3. SPRINKLE the salt, pepper, paprika, and garlic powder on each side of each chicken breast and set aside.

4. HEAT the butter with the canola oil in a large nonstick skillet over medium heat until the butter is melted. Add the chicken and cook it 4 minutes on each side. Place the chicken on top of the rice in the baking dish.

5. ADD the shallots and mushrooms to the same skillet and cook over medium heat, stirring frequently, for 5 minutes.

6. ADD the chicken stock and sherry to the skillet and cook for 3 minutes, stirring constantly.

7. COMBINE the cornstarch and the water in a small bowl. **ADD** the cornstarch mixture to the skillet and stir until the sauce thickens slightly.

8. ADD the rosemary to the skillet, stirring to combine.

9. POUR the sauce over the chicken and rice in the baking dish. Cover the dish with foil and bake for 45 minutes. Serve immediately.

penne with shrimp and feta

Pasta with a zesty Mediterranean flair

Serves 4–6 ✳ *Prep time: 15-20 minutes* ✳ *Cooking time: 25 minutes*

INGREDIENTS

Vegetable oil cooking spray

4 tablespoons olive oil

1 ½ pounds fresh or flash-frozen, deveined shrimp, thawed (see page 159)

½ teaspoon crushed red pepper flakes

1 ½ teaspoons minced garlic

1 ¼ tablespoons lime juice

¾ cup white wine

4 cups canned diced tomatoes, drained

1 teaspoon dried dill or **2 tablespoons** fresh dill, chopped

1 teaspoon dried oregano

Salt and pepper, to taste

8 ounces feta cheese, crumbled (see page 55)

1 pound penne, cooked al dente and drained

1. PREHEAT the oven to 400° F. Coat a 13 x 9 x 2-inch baking pan with cooking spray.

2. HEAT 3 tablespoons of the olive oil in a large skillet over medium heat.

3. ADD the shrimp and red pepper flakes to the skillet and cook for 1 minute, stirring frequently. Use a slotted spoon to transfer the shrimp to the baking pan.

4. HEAT the remaining 1 tablespoon of olive oil in the same skillet over medium heat. Add the garlic and cook for 30 seconds. Add the lime juice, wine, tomatoes, dill, oregano, salt, and pepper and **SIMMER** for 8 to 10 minutes (a few pearl-size bubbles will appear every minute). Remove the skillet from the heat.

5. SPRINKLE the feta cheese over the shrimp in the baking dish. Pour the tomato mixture over the feta-covered shrimp. Bake for 10 to 12 minutes. Remove the dish from the oven.

6. PLACE the penne in a large, warm serving bowl. Add the shrimp mixture to the bowl and toss until all the ingredients are combined. Serve immediately.

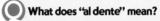

✸ **NOW WHAT?!** ✸

What does "al dente" mean?

This Italian phrase meaning "to the tooth" refers to cooking pasta just until it resists slightly when bitten into.

6 Poultry

Chicken is a mainstay for dinner because it's fast, versatile, and easy to prepare. Why not add a little pizzazz to your meals with these easy gourmet chicken recipes? Choose from Pecan-Crusted Chicken (top), Chicken-Mushroom Quesadillas (middle), or Raspberry Chicken (bottom).

raspberry chicken

Boldly flavored, healthful, and pretty as a picture

Serves 6 ✳ *Prep time: 10 minutes* ✳ *Marinate: 2 hours or overnight* ✳
Cooking time: 35 minutes ✳

INGREDIENTS

Vegetable oil or cooking oil spray

- **6** boneless, skinless chicken breast halves
- ½ **cup** seedless raspberry jam or fruit-only-style raspberry preserves
- ¼ **cup** orange juice
- ½ **cup** frozen pineapple juice concentrate, thawed
- ½ **cup** soy sauce
- **3 tablespoons** raspberry vinegar
- **2** large shallots, minced
- ½ **teaspoon** chili powder
- **1 teaspoon** garlic powder
- ½ **cup** fresh raspberries, mashed with a fork

Garnish (optional):

- ½ **cup** fresh raspberries

1. **COAT** a large glass baking dish with vegetable oil or cooking oil spray.

2. **RINSE** the chicken and pat dry. Place it in the baking dish and set aside.

3. **COMBINE** all the remaining ingredients (except the garnish) in a medium-size bowl.

4. **POUR** the marinade over the chicken and cover the baking dish tightly with foil.

5. **REFRIGERATE** the chicken for 2 hours or overnight.

6. When you're ready to cook, **PREHEAT** the oven to 350° F.

7. **PLACE** the covered baking dish in the oven and bake for 30 minutes.

8. **REMOVE** the baking dish from the oven. Transfer the chicken to a warm serving platter. Pour some of the pan juices over the chicken. Serve the remaining juices in a small bowl if you wish.

9. **GARNISH** the platter with fresh raspberries and serve.

WHAT IS IT AND WHERE DO I FIND IT?

RASPBERRY VINEGAR is voluptuous stuff—milder and fruitier than your usual vinegar and slightly sweet. You'll find raspberry vinegar at most supermarkets or in gourmet shops. Unopened it will keep indefinitely; once opened, raspberry vinegar can be stored in a cool, dark place for up to six months.

What to serve with Raspberry Chicken? Try Sesame Asparagus (page 78) and Lemon-Dill Carrots (page 84).

chicken with honey mustard and basil

A sweet and savory marinade enhances the flavor of grilled chicken

Serves 6 ✳ *Prep time: 15 minutes* ✳ *Marinate: 20 minutes* ✳
Cooking time: 8 minutes

INGREDIENTS

- ⅔ **cup** dry white wine
- ¼ **cup** olive oil
- 3 **cloves** garlic, chopped
- 2½ **tablespoons** Dijon mustard
- 3 **tablespoons** soy sauce
- 3½ **tablespoons** honey
- ⅓ **cup** finely chopped fresh or **2 tablespoons** dried basil
- 6 boneless, skinless chicken breast halves, rinsed and patted dry

1. COMBINE all the ingredients except the chicken in a large shallow dish and whisk until the marinade is thoroughly blended.

2. ADD the chicken breasts to the marinade, turning to coat them thoroughly.

3. MARINATE the chicken at room temperature for 20 minutes. (If you are not going to cook it right away, you can marinate it in the refrigerator for up to 4 hours.)

4. Meanwhile, **PREPARE** a barbecue for medium-heat grilling or preheat the oven broiler.

5. Remove the chicken breasts from the marinade and **TRANSFER** the marinade to a small saucepan. Place it over medium-high heat and bring the sauce to a **BOIL** (nickel-size bubbles will form every few seconds). Boil for 1 minute, then reduce the heat and **SIMMER** the marinade (pearl-size bubbles will form every few seconds) for 2 to 3 minutes, until it is reduced (cooked down) by half.

6. While the marinade is cooking, place the chicken on the grill or broiler pan. **GRILL** or broil the chicken for about 4 minutes per side or until it is cooked through (the juices will run clear when the chicken is pierced through to the center of its thickest part with a fork or skewer).

7. PLACE the chicken on a warm serving platter and pour some of the marinade over it. Serve immediately.

✳ **NOW WHAT?!** ✳

🔵 **How do I select chicken?**

Whether it's a whole bird or chicken parts you're buying, always check the "sell by" date to be sure the bird isn't past its prime. Choose meaty, full-breasted poultry. If there's skin, it should be intact, without bruises. Avoid poultry with an "off" odor or any package that is torn or leaking.

sesame chicken

Grill or bake it—either way it's a snap to prepare

Serves 4-6 ✳ *Prep time: 10 minutes* ✳ *Marinate: 4 hours* ✳
Cooking time: 30 minutes on a grill or 50 minutes in an oven

INGREDIENTS

- ½ **cup** olive oil
- ⅔ **cup** dry sherry (see page 37)
- ½ **cup** soy sauce
- 6 **cloves** garlic, minced
- ¾ **teaspoon** ground ginger or **2 tablespoons** grated fresh ginger
- 1½ **teaspoons** black pepper
- ⅔ **cup** chopped onions
- 1 **tablespoon** grated orange zest (see page 83)
- 4 **tablespoons** sesame seeds
- 2 whole **3-pound** chickens, quartered and rinsed (You can purchase quartered chickens in packages at the supermarket.)

1. **COMBINE** all the ingredients except the chicken in a medium-size bowl and stir well.

2. **PLACE** the chicken quarters in two large resealable plastic bags and divide the marinade evenly between them. Seal the bags and marinate the chicken in the refrigerator for at least 4 hours (or overnight if desired).

3. When you are ready to cook, **PREHEAT** the grill until the coals are very hot or preheat the oven to 450° F. Remove the chicken from the bags, reserving the marinade in a medium-size pan, and place the chicken on the grill or in a large roasting pan.

4. **GRILL** the chicken for 30 minutes, turning it and spooning a few tablespoons of the marinade over it every 4 to 5 minutes. (If you are using an oven, cook the chicken for 45 to 50 minutes, basting it every 8 to 10 minutes.)

5. **TEST** the chicken to see if it's done by piercing the thigh deeply with a skewer or the tip of a sharp, narrow knife. If the juices running out of the puncture are clear (showing no hint of pink), the chicken is done.

6. PLACE the pan of marinade over high heat and bring to a **BOIL** (nickel-size bubbles will form). Boil for 1 minute, then reduce the heat to low and simmer the marinade for 3 minutes.

7. REMOVE the chicken quarters from the grill or the oven and place them on a heated plate. Pour the warm marinade over the chicken and serve. (This dish may also be served at room temperature or cold, after being cooled in the refrigerator.)

* **NOW WHAT?!** *

I've heard that chicken harbors dangerous salmonella bacteria that can make people sick. How can I avoid this?
Wash thoroughly with soap and hot water anything—knives, hands, cutting board, countertop, sink—that comes into contact with raw chicken or its juices. Keep raw chicken refrigerated right up until you use it (preferably not more than one day, and absolutely not more than two days). Never let it sit outside the refrigerator for more than half an hour before cooking. Cook chicken until no red or pink juices run out of the meat when the thickest part is pierced deeply with a fork or skewer. If the juices are tinged with red or pink when tested or if the chicken is still slightly pink inside when it is cut at the table, return it to the grill or broiler and cook it for a minute or two longer.

• • •

How do I baste?
Basting consists of pouring a flavorful liquid—usually a marinade or the liquid drippings from the bottom of the pan—over food while it is roasting, broiling, or grilling. To accomplish this all-important feat, use a spoon, a pastry or barbecue brush, or a bulb baster (a long tube with a bulb on top that sucks in liquid, which can then be squeezed out onto the food). Basting moistens food and adds flavor.

chicken-mushroom quesadillas

A great way to turn leftover chicken into a crowd-pleasing lunch

Serves 6-8 ✳ *Prep time: 20 minutes* ✳ *Cooking time: 20 minutes*

INGREDIENTS

- **3 tablespoons** butter
- **2 tablespoons** vegetable oil
- **4 cloves** garlic, minced
- **1 teaspoon** ground cumin
- **2 teaspoons** chili powder
- **1½ teaspoons** dried oregano
- **5 ounces** (about 1¼ cup) fresh shiitake mushrooms, stemmed and thinly sliced
- **5 ounces** (about 1¼ cup) button or white mushrooms, thinly sliced
- **2 cups** chopped cooked white-meat chicken
- **2½ tablespoons** lime juice
- **¾ cup** thinly sliced red onion
- **½ cup** fresh cilantro
- **2¾ cups** shredded Monterey Jack cheese
- Salt and black pepper to taste
- Olive oil or olive oil cooking spray
- **16** flour tortillas (5½-inch round)

1. PLACE the butter and vegetable oil in a large skillet over medium-high heat. Swirl them together as the butter melts.

2. ADD the garlic, cumin, chili powder, and oregano. Reduce the heat to low and cook for 1 minute, stirring constantly so that the food doesn't burn.

3. ADD the shiitake and button mushrooms. Continue stirring and cooking until the mushrooms are tender, about 10 minutes.

4. REMOVE the skillet from the heat and mix in the chicken, lime juice, onion, and cilantro.

5. COOL the chicken mixture for 10 to 15 minutes, then mix in the cheese and salt and pepper to taste.

6. Meanwhile, **PREPARE** the barbecue grill to medium heat or place a large, heavy skillet on the stove top on medium-high heat.

7. LIGHTLY GREASE one side of each of 8 tortillas with olive oil or olive oil cooking spray and place them, oiled side down, on a large baking sheet.

Serve these Chicken-Mushroom Quesadillas with salsa, and you have a great lunch.

8. DIVIDE the chicken mixture evenly among the tortillas, spreading it over them to within 1 inch of the edges.

9. TOP the chicken mixture with the remaining tortillas, press down and spray with oil.

10. Using a spatula, transfer the quesadillas to the hot grill and **GRILL** the quesadillas until lightly brown, about 3 minutes per side. If using the stove top, place the quesadillas in the skillet one at a time and cook them for 2 to 3 minutes per side, until they are lightly browned; then transfer them to an ovenproof serving platter and keep them in a warm oven while cooking the remaining quesadillas.

11. COOL the quesadillas for 30 seconds, then cut them into wedges using a pizza wheel or sharp knife. Serve immediately.

☀ **NOW WHAT?!** ☀

🔘 **Can I buy chicken that's already cooked?**

Yes. Look for packages of vacuum-packed precooked chicken in the poultry section of your supermarket.

chicken parmesan

An Italian classic that warms the heart

Serves 4-6 ✳ *Prep time: 20 minutes* ✳ *Cooking time: 20 minutes*

INGREDIENTS

- **6** skinless, boneless chicken breast cutlets
- **⅔ cup** seasoned Italian bread crumbs
- **½ cup** grated Parmesan cheese
- **1 teaspoon** dried Italian seasonings
- **1 teaspoon** garlic powder
- **½ teaspoon** black pepper
- **¼ cup** all-purpose flour
- **3** large egg whites
- **2 tablespoons** olive oil
- **3 cups** prepared tomato sauce
- **2 cups** shredded part-skim mozzarella cheese

1. RINSE the chicken cutlets and pat dry with paper towels.

2. COMBINE the next 6 ingredients in a shallow dish and stir the bread-crumb mixture well.

3. PLACE the egg whites in another shallow bowl and use a whisk or fork to beat them until they are slightly foamy.

4. DREDGE the chicken breasts, one at a time, in the bread-crumb mixture. Dip them in egg whites, then again in the bread-crumb mixture.

5. HEAT the oil in a large skillet over medium heat.

6. ADD the chicken breasts, a few at a time, arranging them in the skillet so that they do not touch. Cook the chicken for 5 to 6 minutes on each side or until they are lightly browned.

7. SPOON 1 cup of tomato sauce into a large heatproof ceramic baking dish, covering the bottom with a thin layer. Add the browned chicken breasts and spoon ⅓ cup of tomato sauce over each breast, then top with ⅓ cup of mozzarella cheese.

8. PREHEAT the broiler. Place the dish containing the chicken on a baking sheet.

9. BROIL the chicken for 3 minutes or until the cheese melts.

10. TRANSFER the chicken to a heated platter. Serve immediately.

✳ **NOW WHAT?!** ✳

How do I pound chicken?

To flatten thick chicken breasts, place them between sheets of wax paper or plastic wrap and pound with medium force, using the flat side of a meat mallet (sometimes called a meat tenderizer). If the utensil has two sides, use the flat part instead of the spiky side, which might shred the chicken too much. If you do not have a meat mallet, the bottom of a skillet will do. Carefully wash any surface (including your hands) that touches the raw poultry, since it often carries salmonella bacteria.

• • •

How long will this dish keep?

You can prepare the whole thing ahead of time and simply freeze the finished but uncooked dish. When you are ready to cook, thaw in the refrigerator overnight and broil. Once cooked, it will keep in a sealed container in the refrigerator for up to 2 days.

• • •

I don't have any seasoned Italian bread crumbs. Will plain ones do?

In a pinch, yes, unflavored bread crumbs will do. You can compensate for their plainness by seasoning them with spices. Try adding 1 teaspoon of dried oregano, 1 teaspoon of dried basil, and a dash of salt.

turkey meatloaf

It tastes like old-fashioned meatloaf, but it's much healthier, since it's lower in saturated fats

Serves 6-8 ✳ *Prep time: 15 minutes* ✳ *Cooking time: Approximately 1 hour 10 minutes*

INGREDIENTS

- **2½ pounds** ground turkey
- **1 large** onion, chopped (about **1 ½ cups**)
- **3 cloves** garlic, minced
- **2** extra-large eggs, lightly beaten (or **3** egg whites)
- **2 tablespoons** Worcestershire sauce
- **⅓ cup** white wine
- **¼ cup** plain bread crumbs or **1** slice of bread, torn into small pieces
- **1 ½ teaspoons** salt
- **1 teaspoon** black pepper
- **1 teaspoon** dried thyme
- **⅔ cup** ketchup

1. PREHEAT the oven to 375° F.

2. PLACE all the ingredients except the ketchup in a large bowl.

3. COMBINE the ingredients, using your hands to mix them thoroughly.

4. SPOON the turkey mixture into a 9 x 5 x 3-inch loaf pan. Spread the ketchup evenly over the top of the loaf.

5. BAKE the loaf for 1 hour 10 minutes or until the meatloaf is cooked through (the juices should show no hint of pink when the thickest part of the loaf is pierced deeply with a skewer or a small, sharp knife).

6. TRANSFER the loaf to a heated platter, cut it into slices, and serve. (The meatloaf also can be refrigerated and served cold in a sandwich.)

WHAT IS IT AND WHERE DO I FIND IT?

GROUND TURKEY is now stocked in most supermarket poultry sections as a ground beef alternative. Handle it with the same care you would use for any poultry: Carefully wash your hands, any surface, and any utensil that touches raw poultry, since the meat can contain salmonella bacteria. Buy the freshest package you can and store it in the refrigerator, but never longer than two days. And don't worry too much—cooking thoroughly kills all the bacteria.

✳ NOW WHAT?! ✳

How do I prevent cracks from appearing in my meatloaf?

Before baking the meatloaf, rub the top of it with cold water to smooth the surface and minimize cracking.

• • •

How do I get rid of grease in the meatloaf pan?

Use a bulb baster to remove grease from the pan as the meatloaf bakes. After the meatloaf is cooked, pour any remaining grease into an empty can and throw it away. Don't pour grease down the drain.

chicken with sun-dried tomatoes

A creamy classic that goes beautifully with pasta

Serves 4-6 ✳ *Prep time: 15 minutes* ✳ *Cooking time: 12 minutes*

INGREDIENTS

- **1 cup** yellow cornmeal
- **6** boneless, skinless chicken breast halves, rinsed and cut into 1-inch strips
- **3 tablespoons** unsalted butter
- **2 tablespoons** olive oil
- **3** shallots, minced
- **¾ cup** evaporated skim milk
- **⅔ cup** dry white wine
- **½ cup** chopped rehydrated sun-dried tomatoes (see page 17)
- Salt and black pepper to taste
- **1-2 teaspoons** dried basil or **3 tablespoons** chopped fresh basil

1. **PLACE** the cornmeal in medium-size bowl. Dredge (see page 137) the chicken with the cornmeal until it's coated, shaking off the excess.

2. **PLACE** the butter and oil in a large, heavy skillet over medium heat. Swirl the mixture until the butter melts.

3. **ADD** the chicken pieces to the skillet, a few at a time, and cook over medium heat, turning frequently, for 5 to 6 minutes, until the chicken is lightly browned on both sides. The chicken should be just cooked through (the strips will feel springy when pressed with your finger).

4. Using a slotted spoon, **TRANSFER** the chicken to a warm plate.

5. **ADD** the shallots to the skillet and cook over low heat for 1 minute.

6. **ADD** the evaporated milk, white wine, sun-dried tomatoes, and salt and pepper. Bring the mixture to a **BOIL** (nickel-size bubbles will form every few seconds).

7. REDUCE the heat to low and **SIMMER** (pearl-size bubbles will form every few seconds), stirring frequently, for 4 to 5 minutes or until the sauce thickens.

8. STIR in the basil.

9. RETURN the chicken to the skillet and cook for about 2 minutes or until the chicken is just heated through. Adjust seasonings to taste and transfer the chicken to a warm serving platter. Pour the sauce over it and serve immediately.

Beware of Hidden Treasures

It was my first time roasting a chicken. I got a nice 5-pound chicken, rinsed it, and patted it dry. Then I added some salt and pepper, just like my sister had told me. I put it in a roasting pan and popped it in the oven. When it was done, it looked and smelled great. My girlfriend and I dug in. All was well—until she noticed a piece of plastic. She pulled on it, and out came a plastic bag containing giblets. She told me I was supposed to have removed this before I cooked the chicken. Oh? Next time, I'll look inside and out.

Michael T., Bartlesville, Oklahoma

roast chicken

There's nothing tastier than a plump, perfectly roasted chicken with a light, citrusy gravy

Serves 4-6 ✳ *Prep time: 30 minutes* ✳ *Cooking time: 1 hour 15 minutes*

INGREDIENTS

- **5-** to **6-pound** roasting chicken

Salt and black pepper

- **1 tablespoon** dried thyme or **4 sprigs** fresh thyme
- **1 tablespoon** dried rosemary or **2 sprigs** fresh rosemary
- **1** orange, quartered
- **1** lemon, quartered
- **4 cloves** garlic, peeled
- **2 tablespoons** softened butter

GRAVY

- ¾ **cup** low-sodium chicken broth
- **1 tablespoon** cornstarch
- ¼ **cup** dry white wine
- ½ **cup** orange juice
- ¼ **teaspoon** salt
- ⅛ **teaspoon** pepper

for the chicken

1. PREHEAT the oven to 425° F. Get out a large roasting pan.

2. REMOVE the plastic bag of organs from the chicken's cavity and discard. Rinse the chicken (inside and out) under cold water and pat dry with paper towels.

3. SPRINKLE the cavity of the chicken with salt and pepper. Place the thyme, rosemary, orange, lemon, and garlic inside the cavity and rub them in. **TIE** the legs of the chicken together loosely with kitchen twine to keep the cavity closed.

4. RUB the outside of the chicken with butter and sprinkle the skin with salt and pepper.

5. PLACE the chicken in the roasting pan.

6. ROAST the chicken, basting every 10 to 15 minutes (see page 117), for 1 hour 15 minutes or until the juices run clear when you prick the inside thigh meat deeply with a small, sharp knife. Remove the chicken from the oven when no pink can be detected in the juices. Untie the chicken legs and remove and discard the orange and lemon quarters.

7. TRANSFER the chicken to a warm platter and cover it with an aluminum foil tent to keep it warm while you prepare the gravy.

for the gravy

1. POUR all but 2 teaspoons of fat from the roasting pan into an empty coffee can and discard.

2. ADD the chicken broth to the roasting pan and place it over medium-high heat. Stir for 3 to 4 minutes, deglazing the bottom of the pan (see note at right).

3. In a small bowl, **MIX** the cornstarch with 2 tablespoons of warm broth from the pan. Use a whisk to combine the mixture well, then add it to the pan, blending constantly with the whisk until it is smooth.

4. BRING the mixture to a **BOIL** (nickel-size bubbles will form every few seconds), then reduce the heat so that it **SIMMERS** (pearl-size bubbles will form every few seconds). Stir in the white wine and orange juice.

5. POUR the gravy through a strainer into a gravy bowl. (The strainer will catch any lumps or bits of chicken.) Season it to taste with salt and pepper. Serve with the chicken.

✱ **NOW WHAT?!** ✱

How do I "deglaze" a pan?

Deglazing means adding a little liquid to a pan in which meat or poultry has been cooked, heating it to a boil, and stirring to loosen the browned bits of food still clinging to it. The resulting meaty liquid can be used as a sauce or as a basis for gravy. Before deglazing, pour most of the grease left from cooking into an empty coffee can and discard it. Too much grease will make your gravy or sauce too oily.

pecan-crusted chicken

Moist on the inside, crisp on the outside

Serves 6 ✳ *Prep time: 20 minutes* ✳ *Marinate: 30 minutes* ✳
Cooking time: 30 minutes

INGREDIENTS

MARINADE

3 tablespoons sesame oil

2 tablespoons vegetable oil

2 teaspoons dry sherry

2 tablespoons minced shallots

½ teaspoon grated lemon zest (see page 83)

½ teaspoon grated lime zest (see page 83)

1 tablespoon lemon juice

1 tablespoon lime juice

½ teaspoon black pepper

for the marinade

1. WHISK together all of the ingredients in a small bowl. Set aside.

for the chicken

1. PREHEAT the oven to 450° F.

2. PLACE the chicken breasts in a shallow glass dish. Pour the marinade over the breasts and turn each one to coat it thoroughly. Cover the dish with plastic wrap and refrigerate for 20 to 30 minutes.

3. COMBINE all the remaining ingredients, except the butter, in a blender or the bowl of a food processor. Process the mixture in short bursts until the crackers have turned to crumbs and the pecans are broken into tiny pieces. Pour the crumb mixture into a shallow bowl.

4. GREASE a shallow roasting pan with vegetable oil or cooking oil spray.

5. REMOVE the chicken from the marinade and discard the marinade.

6. COAT both sides of the chicken breasts with the crumb mixture and place them in the roasting pan.

7. DRIZZLE the chicken with the melted butter and place in the oven. Roast for 30 minutes, until the chicken is crisp and browned.

8. REMOVE the chicken from the oven. Transfer it to a warm platter and serve. (The chicken can also be refrigerated and served cold.)

CHICKEN

- **6** skinless, boneless chicken breast halves, rinsed and patted dry
- **I cup** crushed wheat crackers, such as Wheat Thins or Stoned Wheat Thins
- **⅔ cup** grated Parmesan cheese
- **2 teaspoons** dried basil or **¼ cup** chopped fresh basil
- **I teaspoon** dried parsley
- **I teaspoon** garlic powder
- **I teaspoon** black pepper
- **⅔ cup** pecans
- Vegetable oil or cooking oil spray
- **¼ cup** melted butter

Crunchy and bursting with flavor, Pecan-Crusted Chicken makes a lovely dinner. Serve with Wild Rice Salad (see page 60).

7 Meats

Try these hearty favorites for your next main course: Mom's Meatloaf (top), Lamb Chops with Pesto (middle), and Veal Paprika.

caribbean pork tenderloins

The pan drippings provide a nice base for a quick sauce

Serves 6-8 ✳ *Prep time: 15 minutes* ✳ *Marinate: overnight*
✳ *Cooking time: 30 minutes*

INGREDIENTS

- ½ **cup** orange juice
- ½ **cup** lime juice
- ½ **cup** dark rum
- ¼ **cup** pineapple juice
- 6 **cloves** garlic, minced
- 1 large onion, chopped
- 2 **teaspoons** ground ginger
- 2 **teaspoons** dried oregano
- 1 **teaspoon** dried basil
- 2 **teaspoons** dried cumin
- 2 bay leaves, crumbled
- 1 **teaspoon** salt
- 1 **teaspoon** black pepper
- 4 pork tenderloins, **12 ounces** each, rinsed and patted dry
- ½ **cup** chicken broth
- 1 **tablespoon** flour

1. **MIX** the orange juice, ¼ cup of the lime juice, ¼ cup of the dark rum, and all of the next 10 ingredients in a large bowl to make a marinade. Divide the mixture among four large resealable plastic bags.

2. **ADD** a pork tenderloin to each bag and close it securely. Turn the bags so that the pork is coated with the marinade.

3. **REFRIGERATE** the bagged pork loins overnight.

4. When ready to cook, **PREHEAT** the oven to 400°F and remove the pork loins from the bags.

5. **PLACE** the tenderloins in a roasting pan large enough so that the pork loins can fit without touching each other. Discard the marinade.

6. **ROAST** the pork for 25 to 30 minutes or until a thermometer inserted into the center registers 150° F. Remove the pork from the pan and place it on a serving platter. Make a tent with aluminum foil and place it over the pork to keep it warm while it "rests" (see page 133) for a few minutes.

7. While the meat is resting, **PLACE** the roasting pan on top of the stove and turn the heat to medium.

8. ADD the remaining lime juice and rum to the pan. Stir the mixture as it begins to bubble, scraping up the pan drippings from the bottom of the pan.

9. ADD the chicken broth and flour to the pan. Use a whisk to combine the flour mixture thoroughly with the pan drippings mixture. Continue whisking vigorously as the mixture boils (nickel-size bubbles will form every few seconds).

10. COOK 2 minutes at a boil or until the sauce is slightly thickened, whisking to keep it smooth. Remove the sauce from the heat.

11. SLICE the pork into ½-inch-thick slices and serve with some of the sauce drizzled over it. The remainder can be served alongside the meat in a gravy dish.

WHAT IS IT AND WHERE DO I FIND IT?

PORK TENDERLOIN is—big surprise—the most tender cut of pork. (In beef, it's what is called filet mignon.) At the butcher shop or grocery store, choose pork that's pale pink (the older the animal, the darker the meat). It should have a bit of marbling and white (not yellow) fat. When you get the meat home, remove it from the package. Exercise care as with any uncooked meat and wash everything that touches it. Refrigerate it, wrapped loosely in fresh plastic or wax paper, for no more than 2 days.

✷ NOW WHAT?! ✷

🔘 **What does it mean to allow meat to "rest"?**

That's when you delay cutting meat for a few minutes after taking it out of the oven. During this time, the juices settle into the meat fiber. Without this resting period, the juices run out too freely when the meat is cut and some of the flavor leaches away.

• • •

🔘 **I don't have any aluminum foil. Can I let the roast rest uncovered?**

A tinfoil tent keeps the roast from cooling too much while it rests. In a pinch, make a tent from a torn-open paper bag.

beef tenderloin

Simply roast and serve hot, cold, or at room temperature. Do not overcook—it's best when pink

Serves 8 ✳ *Prep time: 15 minutes* ✳ *Cooking time: 40 minutes*

INGREDIENTS

- **2 tablespoons** butter, softened
- **1 3-pound** beef tenderloin, trimmed and tied, at room temperature
- **1 tablespoon** black pepper
- **1 teaspoon** salt

SAUCE

- **1 tablespoon** olive oil
- **1 tablespoon** butter
- **¼ cup** chopped onions or scallions
- **2 tablespoons** minced shallots
- **1 ½ teaspoons** Dijon mustard
- **1 teaspoon** dried parsley or **1 tablespoon** minced fresh parsley
- **¾ cup** dry sherry (see page 37)

1. PREHEAT the oven to 450° F.

2. RUB the butter over the tenderloin, then rub in the pepper and salt. Place in a shallow roasting pan.

3. ROAST the tenderloin for 35 minutes. Remove from the oven and cover the meat with a tinfoil tent. Let the roast stand, or rest, for 10 to 15 minutes before carving.

4. To make the sauce, **HEAT** the olive oil and butter in a small skillet until the butter has melted. **ADD** the onions and shallots to the skillet and cook over medium-high heat, stirring frequently so that the mixture doesn't burn, for about 3 to 4 minutes.

5. ADD the mustard, parsley, and sherry and bring the mixture to a boil (nickel-size bubbles will form every few seconds). Remove the pan from the heat.

6. CARVE the beef into 1-inch-thick slices, dribble some of the sauce over it, and serve.

WHAT IS IT AND WHERE DO I FIND IT?

BEEF TENDERLOIN is a choice, boneless cut taken from along the backbone of the cow. Buy it from a reputable butcher to get the best quality. You might want to purchase a whole tenderloin (6 to 8 pounds prior to trimming) and have the butcher cut half of it for roasting and then slice the rest into 1-inch-thick slabs for steak (filet mignon). Wrap the steaks individually in plastic wrap, then aluminum foil. Label them with the date and place them in the freezer.

☀ NOW WHAT?! ☀

Is trimmed tenderloin better?

You can buy tenderloin untrimmed—with the fat on—or trimmed, with the fat having been removed by a butcher. The price per pound is higher for trimmed, but it's worth it. Before roasting, use kitchen twine or string to tie the meat at intervals of 2 to 3 inches, so that the tenderloin will hold together while roasting and will cook evenly.

FIRST PERSON DISASTER

All Tied Up

Time is money, and I try to conserve both. I have a lot of things on my plate and have to plan everything down to the minute. When I planned a dinner party, my first in a long time, I bought an expensive beef tenderloin and asked the butcher to trim and tie it up for me, in an effort to save time. I prepared it according to the recipe, put it in the oven and had a drink with my guests. We were ready for dinner just as the oven bell chimed. I pulled the beef out and put it on the platter to rest for a few moments while I brought out the already prepared side dishes. I carried in the tenderloin, and my husband cut it into slices and served everyone. We all dug in—that's when I saw the first of my guests gently tugging the twine off her meat. In my haste, I'd forgotten to remove the twine! It had turned brown during cooking and practically blended right into the meat. Clearly, time well spent is more important than being on time.

Pat V., Saratoga, New York

veal paprika

A creamy, soothing, flavorful dish

Serves 6 ✴ *Prep time: 15 minutes* ✴ *Cooking time: 30 minutes*

INGREDIENTS

6 tablespoons canola or vegetable oil

1 ½ pounds veal scallops (¼-inch thick)

1 cup flour seasoned with **1 teaspoon** salt and ¼ **teaspoon** pepper for dredging (see next page)

2 medium onions, thinly sliced

3 cloves garlic, finely minced

2 tablespoons plus **1 teaspoon** sweet paprika

1 ½ cups chicken broth

¾ cup dry sherry (see page 37) or dry white wine

1 ½ cups light sour cream

1 tablespoon lemon juice

Salt and pepper to taste

Garnish (optional): minced fresh parsley

1. **HEAT** 4 tablespoons of the oil in a large skillet over medium heat.

2. **DREDGE** the veal in seasoned flour and cook in batches in the skillet until the meat is lightly browned, 2 to 3 minutes on each side. Place the meat on a serving platter as each batch is browned. Add more oil to the skillet if it seems dry.

3. In the same skillet, **SAUTÉ** the onions (cook over medium-high heat, turning them frequently so that they don't burn) until golden, about 3 to 4 minutes.

4. **ADD** the garlic, paprika, chicken broth, and sherry to the skillet. Bring the mixture to a **BOIL** (nickel-size bubbles will form every few seconds), stirring constantly with a whisk. Add the veal to the skillet and **SIMMER** (pearl-size bubbles will form) for about 5 minutes or until the meat is tender.

5. **STIR** in the sour cream and the lemon juice. Add salt and pepper to taste. Place the veal on a serving plate and pour the sauce over it. Garnish with parsley, if desired, and serve.

Serve Veal Paprika and its savory sauce with Sweet Potato Gratin (see page 88).

WHAT IS IT AND WHERE DO I FIND IT?

SWEET PAPRIKA is a bright orange spice made from finely ground red peppers that can be found in the spice aisle of any supermarket. The most flavorful type comes from Hungary, where foods flavored with paprika are a way of life. To retain the delicate flavor of paprika, keep it in the refrigerator after opening.

✳ NOW WHAT?! ✳

What is "dredging"?

It's coating a food lightly, usually with flour or cornmeal. Either place the coating mixture on a plate and dip the meat in it or put the coating in a large plastic zip-top bag, add the meat in batches, then close and shake the bag.

veal scallops with mushrooms

A dinner party favorite—serve with pasta or rice

Serves 4-6 ✳ *Prep time: 20 minutes* ✳ *Cooking time: 20 minutes*

INGREDIENTS

- 1 ½ **pounds** veal scallops or cutlets
- 1 **teaspoon** salt
- 1 **teaspoon** pepper
- ¼ **teaspoon** cayenne
- 4 **tablespoons** olive oil
- 4 **tablespoons** minced shallots
- 1 **cup** chicken broth
- ⅓ **cup** dry vermouth
- 1 ¼ **cup** sliced fresh mushrooms
- 2 **teaspoons** dried chives
- 1 **tablespoon** dried tarragon
- 1 **tablespoon** dried parsley
- 3 **tablespoons** lemon juice
- 2 **tablespoons** butter

1. For veal scallops, place them between two sheets of plastic wrap and **POUND**, using the flat side of a meat mallet or the back of a heavy skillet, until they are about ⅛-inch thick. Remove the plastic wrap and discard it. If using cutlets, there is no need to pound.

2. **SEASON** the veal with salt, pepper, and cayenne.

3. **HEAT** the oil in a large skillet over medium-high heat. Add the veal to the skillet in batches and **SAUTÉ** each piece for 30 seconds on each side over medium-high heat. Transfer the veal to a warm plate as soon as it turns slightly brown.

4. **ADD** the shallots to the remaining oil and juices in the skillet. Sauté for about 2 minutes over medium-high heat, stirring frequently to prevent scorching.

5. **ADD** the chicken broth to the skillet and scrape up any brown bits with a spatula or wooden spoon, mixing them into the broth. Add all the remaining ingredients except the butter and **SIMMER** (pearl-size bubbles will form every few seconds) until the mixture is reduced by half, about 5 to 7 minutes.

6. **REMOVE** the skillet from the heat and add the butter,

swirling it around until it has melted.

7. RETURN the veal with its juices to the skillet. Turn the veal to coat it with the sauce. Place the veal on a serving platter, drizzle the sauce over it, and serve.

lamb chops with pesto

Equally delicious with homemade or prepared pesto

Serves 6 ✳ *Prep time: 10 minutes* ✳ *Cooking time: 10 minutes*

INGREDIENTS

- **8 tablespoons** plain fat-free yogurt
- **1 cup** prepared or homemade pesto (see below)

Salt and pepper to taste

- **12** lean lamb loin chops on the bone (**3 ounces** each)

HOMEMADE PESTO

- **2 cups** fresh basil leaves, rinsed and thoroughly dried
- **3 cloves** garlic
- **2½ tablespoons** pine nuts
- **½ cup** grated Parmesan cheese
- **2 tablespoons** olive oil

1. STIR the yogurt into the pesto. Add salt and pepper.

2. PREHEAT the broiler or grill. Place the chops on the grill rack or broiler pan and broil them for 4 minutes. Turn the chops over.

3. SPREAD the pesto mixture over the chops and broil for 3 more minutes. (The chops will be medium-rare.) Transfer the chops to a heated platter and serve.

for the homemade pesto

1. PLACE basil, garlic, pine nuts, and Parmesan cheese in a blender or the bowl of a food processor. Blend the ingredients until smooth.

2. ADD the olive oil, 2 teaspoons at a time, and continue blending until all the oil is incorporated.

WHAT IS IT AND WHERE DO I FIND IT?

PESTO is a sauce served over pasta or meat or added to thicken soups. It's made from basil, garlic, and Parmesan or Romano cheese in olive oil, and it is augmented with pine nuts or walnuts. Traditionally, the ingredients are ground together using a mortar and pestle until they form a bright green paste, then olive oil is slowly added to the mixture. Modern food processors make quick work of this chore. Prepared pesto can often be found in refrigerator cases in supermarkets and specialty food stores.

Dress up your lamb chops with delicious pesto sauce. Serve the lamb on the bone or sliced (both ways are shown here).

flank steak

The meat has to marinate overnight, so plan ahead

Serves 6 ✳ *Prep time: 10 minutes* ✳ *Marinate: 12 hours*
✳ *Cooking time: 12 minutes*

INGREDIENTS

- ¾ **cup** soy sauce
- ½ **cup** olive oil
- 4 scallions, minced
- 6 **cloves** garlic, minced
- 2 **teaspoons** ground ginger or **2 tablespoons** grated fresh ginger (see page 39)
- 5 **tablespoons** honey
- 1 **tablespoon** dried rosemary
- 1 **tablespoon** black pepper
- 1 **teaspoon** salt
- 1 **2-pound** flank steak

1. COMBINE all the ingredients except the steak in a large, flat glass or ceramic baking dish.

2. ADD the steak to the marinade mixture and turn it until it is thoroughly coated.

3. COVER the dish tightly with plastic wrap and refrigerate overnight, turning the steak once or twice.

4. When ready to cook, **PREHEAT** a grill or broiler. Remove the steak from the marinade and discard the marinade.

5. GRILL or broil the steak to the desired degree of doneness, about 5 minutes per side for medium-rare.

6. TRANSFER the steak to a cutting surface, cover it with an aluminum foil tent, and let it rest for 5 minutes.

7. SLICE the steak across the grain into thin strips. Serve immediately or keep warm in an oven heated to 200° F.

WHAT IS IT AND WHERE DO I FIND IT?

FLANK STEAK is a boneless cut of beef that's frequently marinated because it is not naturally very tender, although it is quite flavorful (some people consider it the most flavorful cut of beef). An oil-and-vinegar or an oil-and-soy-sauce marinade tenderizes the meat by dissolving some of the connective tissue in its fiber.

✷ NOW WHAT?! ✷

How do I cut flank steak?

Cut it across the grain at a 45-degree angle. If you cut it with the grain, it will be too chewy.

mom's meatloaf

A true blue plate special that's sure to please—and the leftovers are great for sandwiches

Serves 6-8　✳　*Prep time: 20 minutes*　✳　*Cooking time: 1 hour 15 minutes*

INGREDIENTS

- **2 pounds** lean ground beef
- **½ pound** ground pork or veal
- **1 cup** chopped onion
- **2 teaspoons** minced garlic
- **2 eggs,** lightly beaten
- **¼ cup** ketchup or chili sauce
- **¼ cup** bread crumbs or **1 slice** of bread torn into shreds
- **¼ cup** plain nonfat yogurt or skim milk
- **2 tablespoons** Worcestershire sauce
- **2 teaspoons** dried thyme
- **1 teaspoon** dried basil
- **1 teaspoon** dried oregano
- **1 teaspoon** salt
- **1 teaspoon** black pepper

1. PREHEAT the oven to 350° F.

2. COMBINE all the ingredients in a large bowl, using your hands to mix everything together thoroughly.

3. PACK the mixture into a 9 x 5 x 3-inch loaf pan, or shape the mixture into a loaf and place it in a larger baking dish. Pour additional ketchup or chili sauce over the top of the loaf if you wish.

4. BAKE the meatloaf until it is firm to the touch in the center, about 1 hour 15 minutes.

5. TRANSFER the loaf to a platter. Cut it into slices and serve.

WHAT IS IT AND WHERE DO I FIND IT?

BREAD CRUMBS are ground dried bread. You can make your own by toasting stale bread and then grinding it in a blender or food processor. The easier solution is to buy them already prepared. They are sold in canisters—look for them in the condiment or bread section of your supermarket. You can use either plain or seasoned bread crumbs.

For serious comfort food, try a slice of Mom's Meatloaf
with Garlic-Mashed Potatoes (see page 87).

(see page 87)

✷ NOW WHAT?! ✷

Ⓠ How do I prevent the top of my meatloaf from cracking?

Rub water over the top of the loaf before baking.

* * *

Ⓠ Can I use other ground meats besides hamburger?

Meatloaf is any ground meat that has been bound together with eggs or bread crumbs. Any ground meat will do. Try creating combinations with ground beef, veal, pork, and turkey.

meat spaghetti sauce

A homemade hearty tomato sauce to serve over pasta

Serves 8 ✳ *Prep time: 30 minutes* ✳ *Cooking time: 1 hour*

INGREDIENTS

- **2 tablespoons** olive oil
- **3** 4-inch-long sweet Italian sausages (see variations at end of recipe)
- **3** 4-inch-long hot Italian sausages
- **2 pounds** lean ground beef
- **1½ cups** diced onions
- **6 cloves** garlic, minced
- **2 cans (35 ounces** each) Italian plum tomatoes, with juice
- **1 can (28 ounces)** crushed tomatoes, with juice
- **¾ cup** tomato paste
- **¾ cup** dry red wine
- **1 cup** canned tomato sauce
- **3 tablespoons** dried parsley
- **1 tablespoon** dried thyme
- **1 tablespoon** dried oregano
- **2 teaspoons** dried basil
- **1 teaspoon** black pepper
- **1 teaspoon** salt
- **1 pound (16 ounces)** pasta

1. HEAT the olive oil in a large skillet over medium heat.

2. REMOVE the sausages from their casings and break them into small pieces. Add the sausage meat to the pan and cook over medium-high heat, stirring frequently, until browned, about 10 minutes. Transfer the sausage to a colander and drain. Put meat into a large, heavy pot and set aside.

3. ADD the ground beef to the skillet and **COOK** over medium-high heat, breaking the meat into small pieces and stirring it until lightly browned. Using a slotted spoon, transfer the ground beef to the pot with the sausage.

4. ADD the onions and garlic to the skillet and cook over medium heat for 2 to 3 minutes, stirring occasionally. Add them to the pot with the meat.

5. ADD all of the remaining ingredients except the pasta to the pot and bring the mixture to a **BOIL** over medium-high heat (nickel-size bubbles will form every few seconds). Reduce the heat to low and **SIMMER** for 45 minutes to 1 hour (pearl-size bubbles will form every few seconds). Stir the mixture occasionally to prevent the sauce from sticking to the bottom of the pot.

6. COOK the pasta according to the directions on the package while the sauce is simmering. Drain the pasta thoroughly. Transfer it to a large heated bowl or platter and drizzle a little olive oil over it.

7. ADJUST sauce seasonings to taste and pour over the pasta.

Variations: If you don't have sausages handy or don't like them, substitute an additional pound of ground meat.

Add mushrooms, sweet bell peppers, or summer squash to vary the flavor and texture of the sauce.

Pasta with meat sauce is traditionally garnished with freshly grated Parmesan cheese.

Storage tip: Sauce will keep in the freezer for up to 6 months.

WHAT IS IT AND WHERE DO I FIND IT?

ITALIAN SAUSAGES: Sweet Italian sausage is traditionally made from highly seasoned ground pork flavored with garlic and sometimes fennel. Hot Italian sausage is similar, except it also has flakes of hot pepper in the mix. Find both at specialty butcher shops, supermarket meat cases, or Italian grocers. Both types are sold raw and must be cooked thoroughly before eating.

Seafood

So flavorful and so good for you. Try these seafood delights—Shrimp and Leek Stir-Fry (top) and Crab Cakes (bottom).

crab cakes

A healthful version of an all-time favorite

Serves 4-6 ✳ *Prep time: 30 minutes* ✳ *Cooking time: 10 minutes*

INGREDIENTS

- **1 pound** fresh crabmeat, pulled into shreds, or **16 ounces** canned crabmeat (remove any bits of shell; see next page)
- **3 tablespoons** plain nonfat yogurt
- **1½ tablespoons** Dijon mustard
- **2 tablespoons** minced scallions (both white and green parts)
- **1 teaspoon** dried parsley
- **1** large egg, lightly beaten
- **1 teaspoon** salt
- **1 teaspoon** black pepper
- **1-2 dashes** Tabasco
- **6 tablespoons** plain bread crumbs (see page 144)
- **½ -¾ cup** cornflakes, crushed
- **2 tablespoons** olive oil

1. PLACE all of the ingredients except the cornflakes and olive oil in a large bowl and mix them together. Place the cornflakes on a piece of wax paper and crush with a rolling pin. Set aside.

2. SHAPE the crab mixture into 6 large or 12 small cakes.

3. PRESS each side of the cakes into the cornflakes so that they are well coated; as you finish coating them, place each cake on a cutting board or a sheet of waxed paper. (The cakes can be prepared up to this point and kept in the refrigerator for up to 3 hours before cooking; they can be wrapped tightly in plastic wrap, placed in a sealed container, and kept in the freezer for up to 3 weeks.)

4. When ready to cook the crab cakes, **HEAT** the olive oil in a large skillet over medium-high heat.

5. SAUTÉ the cakes (cook over medium-high heat, checking frequently so that the cakes don't burn) for about 5 minutes on each side, pressing down lightly with a spatula. Serve immediately.

✳ **NOW WHAT?!** ✳

🔘 **I don't have cornflakes on hand. Can I use another cereal?**
Yes. Any crisp, flaky cereal that is not sweetened will do.

* * *

🔘 **I don't want to serve the traditional tartar sauce with these cakes. What else would go well with them?**
A little salsa or tomato relish makes a nice garnish for crab cakes.

Crab Cakes are easier to make than most people think. Best of all, you can freeze them before cooking, leaving them for another day; just thaw and cook anytime you want a quick gourmet dinner.

WHAT IS IT AND WHERE DO I FIND IT?

FRESH CRABMEAT: You can find fresh crabmeat in the seafood section of most supermarkets or at your local fish market. It's usually sold by the pound and ready to use. Unless you are using lump crab, you need to pick through the meat with a fork to remove any stray bits of shell.

* * *

PREPARED CRABMEAT is also sold in cans, just like tuna fish. You should pick through the meat before using it and remove any stray bits of shell that may have been left in during processing.

orange-pecan sea bass

Crunchy and citrusy—this dish woos many who shy away from seafood

Serves 4-6 ✳ *Prep time: 10 minutes* ✳ *Cooking time: 8-10 minutes*

INGREDIENTS

- **3 tablespoons** Dijon mustard
- **⅔ cup** orange juice
- **1 teaspoon** dried basil
- **1½ pounds** sea bass fillets
- Salt and pepper to taste
- All-purpose flour, for coating fillets
- **2 tablespoons** butter
- **1 tablespoon** vegetable oil
- **2 tablespoons** orange zest (see next page)
- **⅔ cup** chopped pecans, toasted (see next page)

1. COMBINE mustard, orange juice, and basil in a small bowl. Set aside.

2. SEASON fish fillets with salt and pepper.

3. DREDGE fillets in flour and shake off any excess.

4. MELT butter with oil in a large skillet over medium-high heat.

5. ADD fillets and cook until lightly browned, about 3 to 4 minutes per side.

6. POUR orange juice mixture over fish and stir around fillets, scraping up any browned bits.

7. COVER pan and cook for 5 minutes.

8. TRANSFER to individual plates and sprinkle with orange zest and pecans.

WHAT IS IT AND WHERE DO I FIND IT?

ORANGE ZEST makes a colorful and flavorful addition to a dish. You can't buy zest—you must make it by grating the skin of an orange. Using the back of a cheese grater, grate a freshly washed orange over a plate. The tiny particles are called zest. Avoid scraping into the pith, the white part of the peel—it adds a bitter taste.

✳ NOW WHAT?! ✳

What other fish can be substituted for sea bass?

Snapper or grouper will also work in this recipe.

• • •

How do I toast chopped pecans?

First, chop the pecans. (You don't want to chop them after they're cooked as they will be too hot to handle.) Preheat the oven or toaster oven to 350°F. Place the nuts on a baking pan and toast for 12 minutes, stirring with a wooden spoon every few minutes so that they cook evenly. Keep an eye on them to make sure they don't burn.

grilled swordfish

A lime marinade complements the richness of the fish

Serves 6 ✳ *Prep time: 10 minutes* ✳ *Marinate: 2 to 4 hours*
✳ *Cooking time: 10 minutes*

INGREDIENTS

- ½ **cup** lime juice
- ¾ **cup** dry white wine
- 3 **cloves** garlic, minced
- 2 **tablespoons** Dijon mustard
- ½ **cup** chopped fresh cilantro
- 2 **tablespoons** olive oil
- 1 **teaspoon** black pepper
- 6 swordfish steaks (about ⅓ to ½ **pound** each), 1 inch thick

1. **PLACE** all of the ingredients except the swordfish in a medium-size bowl. Use a whisk to thoroughly blend the marinade.

2. **ARRANGE** the swordfish steaks in a large, shallow glass dish and pour the marinade over them. Cover the dish with plastic wrap and refrigerate for 2 to 4 hours.

3. **PREPARE** a grill or preheat the broiler. Remove the fish from the marinade, reserving the liquid. Grill or broil the steaks for about 4 minutes on each side or until the center is just opaque when you insert a small, sharp knife. Transfer the fish to a warm serving platter.

4. **PLACE** the remaining marinade in a small saucepan over medium heat and **BOIL** (pearl-size bubbles will appear every few seconds) for a full minute.

5. **POUR** some of the cooked marinade over the fish and serve immediately.

❋ NOW WHAT?! ❋

Q Can I cook with leftover wine?

Yes, if it is a dry white wine—which is best with fish—and if it is a good wine. But taste it first to see if it is still palatable. Never cook with any wine or spirit you wouldn't want to drink. Cooking intensifies the taste of wine, so use a good one.

* * *

Q Is it true you should never serve marinade as a sauce?

You should never serve any uncooked marinade as a sauce because it is full of bacteria from the raw food that has been soaking in it. Cooked marinade is another story. To kill any latent bacteria, bring the marinade to a boil and keep it boiling for a full minute before serving.

WHAT IS IT AND WHERE DO I FIND IT?

CILANTRO: Also called fresh coriander, this tangy green herb looks a bit like Italian parsley, but its taste is much more flavorful. You can find it in the produce section of most supermarkets. Look for the freshest bunch because cilantro does not keep long.

baked tuna with sautéed vegetables

An updated version of the traditional "parchment" method of cooking, using aluminum foil instead

Serves 6 ✳ *Prep time: 15 minutes* ✳ *Cooking time: 6 to 8 minutes*

INGREDIENTS

- **3 tablespoons** olive oil
- **3** red bell peppers, seeded and thinly sliced
- **6** cloves garlic, minced
- **2 cups** snow peas, thinly sliced lengthwise, or green beans cut into 1-inch pieces
- **6** scallions (white and green parts), thinly sliced, or **1** small onion, diced
- **1 teaspoon** dried oregano
- **½ teaspoon** dried thyme
- **6** tuna steaks (**8 ounces** each), about 1 inch thick
- **6 sheets** aluminum foil, each measuring 12 x 18 inches
- **3 tablespoons** butter

Salt and black pepper to taste

1. PREHEAT the oven to 425° F.

2. HEAT the oil in a large skillet over medium heat. Add the red pepper and **SAUTÉ** (cooking over medium-high heat, checking frequently so that the peppers don't burn) for 2 minutes.

3. ADD the garlic, snow peas, scallions, oregano, and thyme and sauté for an additional minute. Remove pan from heat.

4. PLACE each of the tuna steaks in the center of a foil sheet. Top the steaks with equal amounts of the cooked vegetables. Place ½ tablespoon of butter on top of the vegetables, then sprinkle with salt and pepper.

5. FOLD the foil over each fish steak, bringing two opposite edges together to make a ridge across the top of the steak. Fold the ridge twice so that it seals the foil packet. Place the packets on a baking sheet.

6. BAKE the fish packets 6 to 8 minutes (for medium-rare tuna). Place the packets on a serving dish or on individual dinner plates. Open the packets slightly to let some of the steam escape. Serve immediately.

Why should tuna be cooked medium-rare?

Although tuna is tender and firm in texture and rich in flavor, it can become gray, chewy, and rather tasteless if cooked too long. It profits from a marinade, even if it is just a squeeze of lemon juice and fresh herbs.

* * *

 I haven't heard of the traditional "parchment" method of cooking. What is it?

Parchment—a paper specially treated for cooking—was once commonly used to make packets in which fish or chicken were steamed along with aromatic herbs and vegetables. The process is often referred to on menus or in cookbooks by the French phrase *en papillote*. Parchment is usually available in cookware specialty shops and some supermarkets.

FIRST PERSON DISASTER

It's All in the Packaging

No sooner had I finished putting the vegetables on top of the fish when the phone rang. It was the car mechanic. The phone is cordless, so I was able to talk while I worked. It turned out that the repair on my car was going to cost twice as much as estimated! I was fuming. I quickly folded up the packets and put them in the oven. Then I called my husband with the bad news. When the oven buzzer beeped, I took the packets out, noticing some burned liquid on the baking sheet. A peek inside revealed the worst part—the vegetables looked totally dried-up and the tuna was ashen. Apparently, I hadn't sealed three of the packets tightly enough, so the fish and vegetables had been baked instead of steamed. I had to laugh—talk about letting off steam! My mom once told me, "Never cook when you're mad." Now I understand why.

Mary Beth M., St. Augustine, Florida

shrimp and leek stir-fry

Sweet and spicy, it's best when made at the last minute

Serves 4-6 ✳ *Prep time: 20 minutes* ✳ *Cooking time: 12 minutes*

INGREDIENTS

- **4 tablespoons** pine nuts
- **4 tablespoons** vegetable oil
- **5 leeks** (white and pale-green parts only), washed well and sliced into thin rounds (see page 77)
- **4 cloves** garlic, minced
- **1 teaspoon** ground ginger or **1 tablespoon** minced fresh ginger (see page 39)
- **3 pounds** large fresh or frozen deveined shrimp, thawed (see next page)
- **⅓ cup** dry sherry
- **⅓ cup** soy sauce
- **⅓ cup** orange juice
- **1 tablespoon** sesame oil
- **1 teaspoon** dried red pepper flakes (omit if you don't like your food spicy)
- **3 cups** cooked white or brown rice

1. PREHEAT the oven to 350°F. Place the pine nuts in a shallow pan and place into the oven for about 5 minutes or until the nuts are lightly toasted. Be sure to watch them carefully or they will burn. Remove from oven and set aside.

2. HEAT the vegetable oil in a skillet over high heat.

3. ADD the leeks and **STIR-FRY** (cooking over high heat, stirring constantly so that the leeks don't burn) for about 3 minutes or until they are just tender.

4. ADD the garlic and ginger and continue stir-frying for about half a minute. Add the shrimp and stir-fry until they turn pink and are heated through, about 1 minute.

5. ADD the sherry, soy sauce, and orange juice to the pan and bring the sauce to a **BOIL** (nickel-size bubbles will form every few seconds).

6. STIR in the toasted pine nuts, sesame oil, and red pepper flakes. Stir-fry for 1 minute and taste. To adjust seasonings, add more soy sauce if you'd like the dish to taste saltier and more sesame oil or sherry if you'd like it to taste sweeter. Serve over rice.

Here's a scrumptious dish for the shrimp lovers in the family.
When served with rice, it's a healthy one-dish meal.

WHAT IS IT AND WHERE DO I FIND IT?

FROZEN, DEVEINED SHRIMP Deveining shrimp is time consuming.
Happily, you can buy flash-frozen shrimp that has already been
deveined. Look for it in your supermarket's frozen seafood section.

salmon with lime mustard

Fast and zesty, it's a healthy treat

Serves 6 ✳ *Prep time: 5 minutes* ✳ *Cooking time: 8-10 minutes*

INGREDIENTS

- **3 tablespoons** coarse-grained mustard (see next page)
- **3 tablespoons** lime zest (see page 83)
- **3 tablespoons** lime juice
- **2 teaspoons** minced garlic
- **½ teaspoon** salt
- **¾ teaspoon** black pepper
- **6** salmon fillets (**6 ounces** each, with skin on)

Vegetable oil or cooking oil spray

1. PREHEAT the broiler or grill to its highest setting.

2. COMBINE all of the ingredients except the salmon in a medium-size bowl.

3. GREASE the broiler pan with vegetable oil or cooking oil spray until it is generously coated. **PLACE** the salmon fillets, skin side down, on the grill or pan.

4. BRUSH the top of each fillet with the mustard mixture.

5. BROIL or grill the fillets—do not turn them—for 8 to 10 minutes or until the center of each fillet is still slightly pink.

6. SERVE immediately.

WHAT IS IT AND WHERE DO I FIND IT?

FRESH SALMON is sold whole or cut into steaks or fillets. Buy the freshest fish you can find in a busy fish market that has a lot of turnover. When making a simple recipe such as this one, cook double the amount of salmon you will need and refrigerate the extra portion. It's wonderful when served over salad greens a day or two later or cut into chunks and tossed with hot pasta, dill, and olive oil.

* * *

COARSE-GRAINED MUSTARD is mustard with mustard seeds in it. Smooth mustards have pulverized seeds, so you can't see them. Grainy mustards are usually spicier than the smoother Dijon-style mustards.

✴ NOW WHAT? ✴

I don't have any coarse-grained mustard. Can I substitute something else?

Yes, any type of Dijon mustard will work. But the stuff you put on hot dogs won't do.

* * *

I'd like to use salmon steaks instead of fillets. What's the difference?

A salmon steak is horseshoe-shaped, thicker than a fillet, and has skin around its sides and bones. It also contains bones, unlike the fillet. A salmon fillet is much thinner and has no real edge. It will have skin on one side. In this recipe, you can substitute a steak for a fillet.

ginger-sesame salmon

Fish with an Asian flair in a foil packet

Serves 6 ❋ *Prep time: 15 minutes* ❋ *Cooking time: 18 minutes*

INGREDIENTS

1 ¼ **cups** thinly sliced leeks or **1** large onion, sliced and separated into rings

3 medium carrots, shredded

1 yellow bell pepper, seeded and cut into thin strips

1 red bell pepper, seeded and cut into thin strips

6 **sheets** aluminum foil, measuring 12 x 18 inches each

6 salmon fillets (**6 ounces** each)

1 **teaspoon** ground ginger or **1 tablespoon** grated fresh ginger (see page 39)

1 **teaspoon** garlic powder

3 **tablespoons** rice-wine vinegar or white vinegar

3 **tablespoons** sherry

3 **teaspoons** sesame oil

Salt and pepper to taste

1. **PREHEAT** the oven to 450°F or preheat a grill to its highest setting.

2. **PLACE** the leeks, carrots, and yellow and red peppers on the foil sheets, dividing the vegetables evenly.

3. **PLACE** one salmon fillet atop each mound of vegetables.

4. In a small bowl, **MIX** the ginger, garlic powder, vinegar, sherry, and sesame oil.

5. **DRIZZLE** the ginger mixture evenly over the tops of the salmon fillets. Season with salt and pepper.

6. **FOLD** the foil over each fillet, bringing the two opposite edges together to make a ridge across the top of the steak. Fold the ridge twice so that it seals the foil packet. Place the packets on a baking sheet.

7. **BAKE** the packets for 18 minutes or grill them for 15 minutes on a covered grill.

8. **REMOVE** the packets from the oven or grill. Carefully open the packets part of the way, allowing the steam to

escape, then open them fully. Transfer the fish and vegetables from each of the foil packets onto individual plates. Serve immediately.

RICE-WINE VINEGAR, used in Asian cooking, has a smooth, mild flavor. Look for it near the other vinegars in the salad dressing section of your supermarket.

* * *

SESAME OIL, another ingredient that comes from Asia, is made from pressing sesame seeds. It's also available in most supermarkets. It should be refrigerated after opening.

✸ NOW WHAT?! ✸

 How can I avoid burning my fingers when I open a packet?

Burns occur when a packet (or pot, for that matter) in which food has been steamed is opened quickly and a large amount of steam rushes out all at once. After cooking with the packets, carefully open a small part of the seal, keeping your hands on each side of the opening instead of over it and your face turned away from it. Wearing kitchen mitts or gloves can also help. After some of the steam has escaped from the small opening, gradually open the rest of the seal.

scallop and mushroom sauté

Last-minute cooking, melt-in-your-mouth taste

Serves 6-8 ✳ *Prep time: 15 minutes* ✳ *Cooking time: 8-10 minutes*

INGREDIENTS

- **2 pounds** bay scallops
- **1 cup** dry white wine or vermouth
- **2 tablespoons** lemon juice
- **2 tablespoons** butter
- **2 tablespoons** olive oil
- **1 pound** button or shiitake mushrooms, thinly sliced
- **½ cup** diced onion
- **1 teaspoon** dried oregano
- **1 teaspoon** arrowroot (see next page), or **2 teaspoons** cornstarch
- **3 tablespoons** cold water
- **1 teaspoon** dried parsley
- **2 tablespoons** grated Parmesan cheese

Salt and pepper to taste

1. PLACE the scallops, wine, and lemon juice in a large skillet over medium-low heat. **SIMMER** the scallops (pearl-size bubbles will form every few seconds) for 1 to 2 minutes, just until the scallops become opaque. Do not overcook or the scallops will become tough.

2. DRAIN the liquid from the skillet into a small bowl and set it aside. Transfer the scallops to another small bowl and set them aside.

3. RETURN the skillet to the stove. Melt the butter and oil over low heat. Add the mushrooms and onion. Increase the heat to medium-high and cook for 3 to 5 minutes, stirring occasionally. Add the oregano and thoroughly stir to combine the mixture.

4. RETURN the scallops to the pan and stir to combine. Transfer the scallop-mushroom mixture to a warm bowl and set aside.

5. In a small bowl, **MIX** the arrowroot and water together. Add this to the skillet and stir. Add the reserved cooking liquid, plus the parsley, Parmesan cheese, and seasonings, stirring to combine thoroughly. Let the mixture simmer for about 2 minutes, stirring constantly, until the sauce is smooth and slightly thickened.

6. ADD the scallop-mushroom mixture to the skillet. Heat for 1 minute, until it is warm. Transfer to a warm platter and serve immediately.

ARROWROOT, available in supermarkets and natural food stores, is a fine powder used as a thickening agent. It thickens at a lower temperature than flour or cornstarch, and its flavor is much more subtle. But it will lump unless you mix it with a little cold liquid before adding it to a hot mixture.

✳ NOW WHAT? ✳

My scallops are always tough. What am I doing wrong?
You are probably cooking them too long. Barely cooking them gives the freshest-tasting, most tender results.

* * *

I can only get sea scallops. Can I use them in this recipe?
Yes, but you will need to pat them dry with a paper towel before cooking to remove any excess water. Also, cook them just a bit longer, up to 3 minutes, depending on their size.

* * *

What can I serve with this recipe to soak up the pan juices?
These pan juices go well over brown or white rice or pasta such as bowties, penne, or fusilli.

rosemary shrimp

A delicacy ready in less than 15 minutes

Serves 4-6 ✳ *Prep time: 5 minutes* ✳ *Cooking time: 6-8 minutes*

INGREDIENTS

5 tablespoons olive oil

½ **cup** minced yellow onion

2 cloves garlic, minced

2 teaspoons dried rosemary, crumbled, or **2 tablespoons** minced fresh rosemary

1¾ **pounds** large fresh or frozen deveined shrimp (see page 159), thawed

⅔ **cup** dry white wine

Salt and pepper to taste

1. HEAT the oil in a large skillet over high heat.

2. ADD the onion, garlic, and rosemary and **SAUTÉ** (cooking over medium-high heat, checking frequently so that the food doesn't burn), stirring occasionally, for about 2 minutes.

3. ADD the shrimp and continue sautéing until it is heated through, about 2 minutes.

4. ADD the wine and continue sautéing for another minute, stirring constantly.

5. SEASON with salt and pepper to taste. Serve immediately.

WHAT IS IT AND WHERE DO I FIND IT?

FRESH ROSEMARY, a highly aromatic herb, is usually used chopped or snipped (cut with scissors) because its needlelike leaves are rather stiff. Look for it among the fresh herbs in the produce section of your supermarket.

✳ NOW WHAT? ✳

🔘 **What's a good side dish for Rosemary Shrimp?**
Wild Rice Salad (page 60) is a great complement to the rosemary and the shrimp.

grilled tuna with fruit salsa

Summer fruit is the perfect complement to tuna

Serves 4 ✳ *Prep time: 8 minutes* ✳ *Cooking time: 8 minutes*

INGREDIENTS

- ¾ **cup** coarsely chopped honeydew melon
- ¾ **cup** coarsely chopped cantaloupe
- 2 small peaches, peeled and chopped
- 1 **cup** chopped red onion
- 2 **tablespoons** dried parsley
- ¼ **cup** chopped fresh or 1 tablespoon dried cilantro
- 3 **tablespoons** olive oil
- 3 **tablespoons** lime juice
- 4 fresh tuna steaks (**6 ounces** each), about 1 inch thick

1. **PREPARE** the grill so that the heat is medium-high, or preheat the broiler.

2. To make the salsa, **COMBINE** the honeydew, cantaloupe, peaches, onion, parsley, cilantro, 2 tablespoons of the olive oil, and all of the lime juice in a medium-size bowl. Set this aside.

3. **BRUSH** the tuna steaks with the remaining olive oil.

4. **GRILL** or broil the tuna for about 3 to 4 minutes per side or until the flesh is still pink in the middle when a slender knife is inserted into the center of the steak.

5. **TRANSFER** the steaks to warm dinner plates and spoon the salsa (see above, step 2) alongside them. Serve immediately.

🔵 **If I use a broiler instead of a grill, do I cook the fish any differently?**

Everything is the same, including the cooking time.

✳ ✳ ✳

🔵 **If I can't find a ripe melon in the market, can I substitute something else?**

Yes. Fruits such as nectarines, papayas, and mangoes will work well as substitutes. Or simply add them to the mixture for a little variety.

WHAT IS IT AND WHERE DO I FIND IT?

MELONS are the pride of produce sections and farmers' stands, especially in the summer when they are at their best. If fully ripe, a melon can be kept in the refrigerator for up to 5 days. Store underripe melons at room temperature, preferably in a paper bag pierced with several holes, until they ripen. Adding an apple to the bag will speed the process.

Desserts

Indulge yourself with these award-winning desserts (from top to bottom, left to right): Carrot Cake, Quick Cheesecake Tart, Old-Fashioned Lime Pie, and Oatmeal Raisin Cookies.

ginger cookies

Soft, chewy morsels with plenty of spice

Yields: 30 cookies ✳ *Prep time: 20 minutes* ✳ *Chilling time: 1 hour*
✳ *Cooking time: 10-12 minutes*

INGREDIENTS

2 cups all-purpose flour

2½ teaspoons ground ginger

1½ teaspoons ground cinnamon

1 teaspoon ground cloves

¼ teaspoon ground allspice

2 teaspoons baking soda

½ teaspoon salt

¾ cup crystallized ginger (see next page), chopped

1 cup plus **2 tablespoons** dark brown sugar, packed

½ cup vegetable shortening (see next page), room temperature

¼ cup sweet (unsalted) butter, softened

1 large egg, lightly beaten

¼ cup molasses (see next page)

Vegetable oil or cooking oil spray

Confectioners' sugar for coating

1. **COMBINE** the first 7 ingredients in a medium-size bowl and stir until they are blended.

2. **ADD** the crystallized ginger to the flour mixture and set the bowl aside.

3. Using an electric mixer, **BEAT** the brown sugar, shortening, and butter in a large mixing bowl until the mixture is smooth and creamy.

4. **ADD** the egg and molasses to the sugar mixture and beat until thoroughly blended.

5. **ADD** the flour mixture to the sugar and egg mixture, ⅓ at a time, stirring to combine them.

6. **COVER** the bowl and refrigerate for at least 1 hour. (You may refrigerate the dough overnight if you wish.)

7. **PREHEAT** the oven to 350°F. Grease two cookie sheets lightly with vegetable oil or cooking oil spray. Spoon the sugar for dusting onto a small plate and set aside.

8. SHAPE the cookie dough into 1-inch balls by rolling them in the palm of your hand. When done, roll the balls in sugar until they are completely coated. Place the balls on the cookie sheets about 2 inches apart so that the cookies can spread during baking.

9. BAKE the cookies just until cracks appear on their tops, about 10 minutes. The cookies should still be slightly soft. Remove from the oven and allow them to cool on the baking sheets for 5 minutes.

10. TRANSFER the cookies to wire racks and allow them to cool completely. Serve or store in a zip-top plastic bag in the freezer.

WHAT IS IT AND WHERE DO I FIND IT?

CRYSTALLIZED GINGER: Available in most supermarkets, it is made by cooking fresh ginger in sugar syrup and coating it with coarse sugar. The dried, powdered ginger is far less potent and should not be substituted for crystallized ginger in this recipe.

* * *

MOLASSES: Most supermarkets carry this sweetener, which is made from the juice pressed from sugarcane that has been slowly cooked until much of the moisture has evaporated; its syrup is dark and very thick. Light or dark molasses can be used in this recipe; the dark kind imparts a more robust flavor.

* * *

VEGETABLE SHORTENING: This is a solid fat that gives the ginger cookie its traditional texture. Substituting butter or liquid vegetable oil in this recipe is not recommended.

* **NOW WHAT?!** *

I've seen "blackstrap" molasses in stores. Is it good for this recipe?

Yes. It's very thick and dark and somewhat bitter tasting due to a longer cooking process. It will give the cookies a stronger flavor.

* * *

Why mix the butter and sugar, then the eggs, then the dry ingredients? Why not just dump all the ingredients in together?

Butter and sugar tend to lump and separate if egg (a binding agent) is added before they are creamed together. The minute dry ingredients such as baking powder and soda get wet, they will start working to release the gases that make the cookies rise. Mixing them first with the flour allows them to be added evenly to the wet ingredients, so the cookie batter rises more evenly.

oatmeal raisin cookies

Chewy and buttery and full of plump raisins

Yields: 36 cookies ✳ *Prep time: 30 minutes* ✳ *Cooking time: 10 minutes*

INGREDIENTS

Vegetable oil or cooking oil spray

- ¾ **cup** sweet (unsalted) butter, room temperature
- I **cup** plus **2 tablespoons** light brown sugar, packed
- ½ **cup** granulated sugar
- I egg plus I egg white, lightly beaten
- ½ **cup** low-fat milk
- I ½ **teaspoons** vanilla extract
- 3 **cups** quick-cooking rolled oats
- I ¼ **cups** all-purpose flour
- ½ **teaspoon** baking soda
- ½ **teaspoon** salt
- I ¼ **cup** raisins

1. PREHEAT the oven to 350° F. Lightly grease four cookie sheets (also called baking sheets) with vegetable oil or cooking oil spray.

2. Using an electric mixer, **BEAT** the butter and sugars in a large mixing bowl, until the mixture is smooth and creamy. Set the bowl aside.

3. COMBINE the eggs, milk, and vanilla in a small mixing bowl. Add the raisins and stir until the raisins are coated. Set the bowl aside.

4. In a medium-size bowl, **STIR** together the oats, flour, baking soda, and salt.

5. ADD the raisin mixture to the butter mixture and stir until they are combined.

6. ADD the flour mixture to the wet mixture, ⅓ at a time, stirring just enough to combine the two mixtures.

7. DROP large teaspoonfuls of the batter onto the cookie sheets, spacing the drops about 2 inches apart, to allow them to spread during baking.

8. BAKE the cookies for about 10 minutes or until they are golden brown. Remove the cookies from the oven and let them cool on the pans for about 5 minutes.

9. TRANSFER the cookies to wire racks and allow them to cool completely. Serve immediately or store in a zip-top plastic bag in the freezer for up to a month.

✳ **NOW WHAT?!** ✳

Q Some of my cookies are done before the others. Why?
Most ovens have some spots that are hotter than others, so the cookies may not bake evenly. To even up the process, rotate the baking sheets front to back and top to bottom during baking. The shelves should be about six inches apart to ensure proper air circulation.

* * *

Q What if I like nuts in my oatmeal raisin cookies?
Stir in 1/2 to 1 cup of chopped pecans or walnuts after the flour mixture has been added (step 6, previous page).

* * *

Q I've heard cooks talk about "creaming" ingredients. What does that mean?
When butter and sugar are mixed together, they take on a creamy texture (step 2, previous page) and are said to be "creamed" together. The process can be done by hand, but it is laborious. Using an electric mixer is the easier way.

OATS: The rolled variety—steamed, flattened, and cut into flakes—can be found in any supermarket. They're what you use to make oatmeal. Quick-cooking or regular rolled oats are interchangeable in this cookie recipe. But don't use the instant variety, since it has been precooked and will turn lumpy. Also avoid steel-cut oats, also called Scotch- or Irish-style oats. They take far too long to cook to be suitable for this cookie recipe.

Plump Oatmeal Raisin Cookies—a delectable afternoon treat

apple pie

Granny Smith apple filling and a homemade pie crust—
pure comfort food, especially when topped with ice cream

Serves 6-8 ✳ *Prep time: 30 minutes* ✳ *Cooking time: 1 hour*

INGREDIENTS

- **3 cups** all-purpose flour
- **I teaspoon** salt
- **I cup** cold sweet (unsalted) butter, cut into small pieces
- **6 (or more) tablespoons** ice water
- **3 tablespoons** lemon juice

or

- **I** prepared **9-inch** pie shell with top crust, unbaked

PIE FILLING

- **¼ cup** granulated sugar
- **2 tablespoons** flour
- **¼ teaspoon** ground nutmeg
- **I teaspoon** ground cinnamon
- **2 tablespoons** lemon juice
- **10** Granny Smith apples, peeled, cored, and thinly sliced (see next page)
- **2 tablespoons** sweet (unsalted) butter, cut into small pieces

for the crust

I. COMBINE flour and salt in a medium-size bowl. **ADD** the butter and mix it into the flour mixture with a fork or your fingers. (Or combine in a food processor fitted with a metal blade.) When the mixture resembles oatmeal, **ADD** water and lemon juice a little at a time, until the dough just holds together. **DIVIDE** the dough in half. Shape each half into a ball, wrap each in plastic wrap, and place in the freezer for 15 minutes.

2. Remove the dough from the freezer. On a lightly floured surface, **ROLL** one dough ball into a circle about 2 inches larger than the pie pan; this is the bottom crust. Roll the other ball into a circle about half an inch larger than the pan; this is the top crust. Work quickly and try to handle the dough as little as possible.

3. ARRANGE the bottom crust in an 8- or 9-inch pie pan. The edge of the crust should slightly overlap the rim of the pan slightly. Place the top crust on a plate. Cover the crusts with wax paper and place in the refrigerator while you prepare the pie filling.

for the pie

1. PREHEAT the oven to 400°F.

2. COMBINE the sugar, flour, nutmeg, cinnamon, and lemon juice in a small bowl.

3. PLACE the sliced apples in a large bowl. Add the sugar mixture and toss until the slices are evenly coated. Take the pie crusts out of the refrigerator and **ARRANGE** the apples in layers in the pan. Scatter the butter pieces over the apples.

4. PLACE the top crust over the apples. Trim the edge with a knife and discard the excess crust. Seal the crusts together by pressing down all around the edges with a fork or your fingers. Using a sharp knife, poke 6 ½-inch-long slits in the top crust.

5. BAKE pie until the crust is very lightly browned, about 1 hour. If the edges brown too quickly, lay strips of aluminum foil around them and leave in place for the remainder of the baking time.

6. REMOVE the pie from the oven. Place it on a wire rack and let cool for 10 minutes. Serve the pie warm with vanilla ice cream.

✳ **NOW WHAT?!** ✳

🔵 **Why does the recipe say that pie dough should not be handled too much?**

Overhandling pie dough tends to make the finished crust tough or less flaky. Adding too much liquid can also toughen the crust. As you practice making pie dough by making more pies, you will find you are able to use smaller amounts of liquid and you will gradually handle the dough less and less.

• • •

🔵 **How do I keep apples from turning brown after I slice them?**

Warm air will turn cut fruit brown. Stop the browning by keeping your just-sliced apples in a bowl of cold water. You can also sprinkle them with lemon juice.

WHAT IS IT AND WHERE DO I FIND IT?

GRANNY SMITH APPLES: Most produce sections in supermarkets and greengrocers carry these tart, green apples that are perfect in pies. Don't substitute other apple varieties for Granny Smiths unless you know that they are recommended to be used in pies.

chocolate midnight pie

Like a dense fudge brownie in pie form—totally decadent!

Serves 8 ✳ *Prep time: 15 minutes* ✳ *Cooking time: 25 minutes*

INGREDIENTS

Vegetable oil or cooking oil spray

½ **cup** butter

2½ **squares** unsweetened chocolate (**2**½ **ounces**)

2 large eggs, lightly beaten

1 **cup** sugar

¼ **cup** plus **1 teaspoon** flour

¼ **teaspoon** salt

1 **teaspoon** vanilla

Garnish (optional): fresh raspberries and whipped cream, or vanilla ice cream

1. PREHEAT the oven to 350°F. Grease a 9-inch-wide glass pie dish with vegetable oil or cooking oil spray and set aside.

2. MELT the butter and chocolate in a small saucepan over very low heat, stirring frequently so that the chocolate does not burn. When the mixture is smooth, remove it from the heat and set aside.

3. Using an electric mixer, **BEAT** the eggs and sugar in a medium-size bowl for about 3 minutes. Add the warm chocolate mixture to the bowl. Then add the flour, salt, and vanilla. Mix thoroughly until the mixture is smooth.

4. POUR the mixture into the pie dish.

5. BAKE the pie for 25 minutes. Remove the pie from the oven and allow it to cool slightly. Garnish with fresh raspberries and whipped cream or vanilla ice cream and serve warm or at room temperature.

Add whipped cream and fresh raspberries and turn this simple chocolate pie into an elegant, delicious dessert.

WHAT IS IT AND WHERE DO I FIND IT?

UNSWEETENED CHOCOLATE is chocolate without any added sugar. Available in supermarkets, it is ideal for cooking because you can add as much or as little sweetening as your recipe calls for. You might want to experiment with imported chocolates, available in some specialty food shops, since the flavor of each country's chocolate differs slightly.

✴ NOW WHAT?! ✴

Q Whenever I melt chocolate, it forms together. Why?

Although chocolate can be melted together with other ingredients such as butter or a liqueur, a single drop of water will cause it to "seize" (clump and harden). Sometimes you can correct seizing immediately by adding vegetable oil to the chocolate (1 tablespoon of a neutral-tasting oil such as canola oil per 6 ounces of chocolate), and stirring the mixture slowly over very low heat until it is smooth.

* * *

Q I can't seem to melt chocolate without it taking on a bitter taste. Why?

You melted it over heat that was too high, so it scorched. Very low heat and constant stirring is needed to melt chocolate slowly and to prevent it from burning.

old-fashioned lime pie

A cool summertime dessert

Serves 8 ✳ *Prep time: 30 minutes* ✳ *Cooking time: 30 minutes*
✳ *Chilling time: 3 hours*

INGREDIENTS

- **5 ounces** vanilla wafer cookies
- **½ stick** sweet (unsalted) butter, melted
- **1½ tablespoons** lime zest (see page 83)
- **¼ teaspoon** ground cinnamon
- **1 can (14 ounces)** sweetened condensed milk (see next page)
- **¾ cup** lime juice
- **2** extra-large eggs, beaten lightly

Garnish (optional): Whipped cream

1. PREHEAT the oven to 350°F.

2. GRIND the vanilla wafers in a blender or the bowl of a food processor fitted with a steel blade. Add the melted butter, 1 teaspoon of the lime zest, and the cinnamon. **PROCESS** the crumb mixture for a few additional seconds, until it is thoroughly moist. Transfer the crumb mixture to an ungreased 9-inch glass pie pan and firmly press the mixture into the bottom and up the sides of the dish.

3. BAKE the crumb crust for about 10 minutes, until golden brown. Remove the crust from the oven.

4. PLACE the condensed milk, lime juice, and remaining lime zest in a medium-size bowl and use a whisk to mix them together. Add the eggs and whisk the filling mixture until it is slightly frothy.

5. POUR the filling into the warm crust. Bake the pie for 20 minutes or until the filling sets. Cool the pie slightly, about 15 minutes, or until the glass pan is barely warm.

6. REFRIGERATE the pie for at least 3 hours. (Or cover it with plastic wrap and refrigerate it for several days.)

7. REMOVE the pie from the refrigerator just before serving. Cut into wedges and serve plain or topped with whipped cream.

WHAT IS IT AND WHERE DO I FIND IT?

SWEETENED CONDENSED MILK: This is canned whole milk that is very thick, since 60 percent of its water has been removed and sugar has been added. Don't try to substitute regular condensed milk or plain milk; the pie owes its silky texture to this particular product. You can find it in the baking section of most supermarkets.

❋ **NOW WHAT?!** ❋

🔵 **Does it matter if you bake a pie in a glass pan or an aluminum one?**
Each type of pie dish or pan has its own special use, so it is best to use the one your recipe calls for. Glass pie dishes, as well as dark-metal and dull-metal pans, absorb heat and produce a crisp, golden-brown crust, while shiny aluminum pans produce a pale crust. (If you substitute a glass pie dish in a recipe that calls for another type of pie pan, lower the baking temperature by 25° F.)

Lime pie is light and tart. It makes an ideal ending to a barbecue or grilled fish dinner.

chocolate mousse cake

Fabulous and so easy to make. Plan ahead—it must be chilled for two hours

Serves 8-10 ✳ *Prep time: 30 minutes* ✳ *Cooking time: none* ✳ *Chilling time: two hours*

INGREDIENTS

- **9 ounces** chocolate wafer cookies
- **8 tablespoons (1 stick)** sweet (unsalted) butter, melted
- **¼ teaspoon** ground cinnamon
- **2 cups (12 ounces)** semi-sweet chocolate chips
- **2 cups** whipping cream
- **Garnish** (optional): fresh mint leaves and/or grated chocolate

1. GRIND chocolate wafers in a blender or food processor fitted with a steel blade. Transfer the crumbs to a small bowl and stir in the melted butter and cinnamon. Press the mixture into the bottom of a 9-inch springform pan. Place the crust in the refrigerator while making the filling.

2. MELT the chocolate chips in a microwave-proof dish on high for 3 to 4 minutes or in a small saucepan over very low heat, stirring frequently to prevent scorching. Remove the melted chocolate from the heat. Allow the chocolate to cool slightly.

3. POUR the whipping cream into a mixing bowl and beat with an electric mixer until soft peaks form.

4. Using a rubber spatula, **FOLD** the melted chocolate into the whipped cream. Stir until the ingredients are thoroughly combined and the color is uniform.

5. POUR the mixture into the crumb crust and refrigerate for 2 hours.

6. When ready to serve, **LOOSEN** the sides of the cake using a sharp knife. Release the spring, remove the sides of the springform pan, and slide the cake, bottom still attached, onto a serving plate.

7. GARNISH the cake with fresh mint leaves and/or grated chocolate.

✳ **NOW WHAT?!** ✳

🔘 **Can other forms of chocolate be substituted for the chips?**

You can use semisweet chocolate bars or squares. You will need 1⅓ cups of melted chocolate. Do not use baker's squares, since they are too bitter.

∗ ∗ ∗

🔘 **How do I use a springform pan?**

This clever two-part cake pan has a flat bottom and a collar with a spring-release clip that holds the sides. When you release the clip, the sides spring away from the edges of the cake. (Before removing the springform sides, run a knife around the edge between the cake and the collar.) The bottom of the pan can be left in place and used as a serving plate.

carrot cake

This very moist, flavorful cake will keep in the refrigerator for up to a week

Serves 8 to 10 ✳ *Prep time: 40 minutes* ✳ *Cooking time: 50 minutes*

INGREDIENTS

- **2 cups** all-purpose flour
- **2 teaspoons** baking powder
- **1½ teaspoons** baking soda
- **½ teaspoon** salt
- **2¼ teaspoons** ground cinnamon
- **1 teaspoon** ground ginger
- **1¾ cups** sugar
- **1½ cups** vegetable oil
- **4 large** eggs
- **2½ cups** grated carrots
- **½ cup** chopped walnuts
- **1 cup** plus **2 tablespoons** crushed pineapple, drained (save the juice for the icing)

CREAM CHEESE ICING

- **1 pound** reduced-fat cream cheese, softened
- **½ cup** unsalted butter, softened
- **2½ teaspoons** vanilla extract
- **2¾ cups** confectioners' sugar
- **3 tablespoons** pineapple juice

for the cake

1. PREHEAT the oven to 350°F. Spray two 9-inch round cake pans with cooking spray.

2. PLACE the flour, baking powder, baking soda, salt, cinnamon, and ginger in a large bowl and stir until combined.

3. PLACE the sugar, oil, and eggs in another large mixing bowl. Using an electric mixer, beat them together for about 5 minutes, until the mixture is smooth.

4. STIR in the carrots, walnuts, and pineapple. Stir in the flour mixture.

5. POUR equal amounts of cake batter into the pans and bake for 45 to 50 minutes, until a wooden toothpick inserted into the center of one of the cake layers comes out clean.

6. REMOVE pans from the oven and place them on a wire rack to cool for 15 minutes. Then remove the cake layers from the pans and put them on the rack to finish cooling.

Luscious cream cheese frosting makes this tantalizing carrot cake a mouthwatering treat.

for the icing

1. PLACE the cream cheese, butter, and vanilla in a large mixing bowl. Using an electric mixer, beat them together for about 2 minutes, until the mixture is smooth and creamy.

2. BEAT the confectioners' sugar into the cream cheese mixture, scraping down the sides of the bowl to make sure that the ingredients are combined thoroughly.

3. ADD the pineapple juice, 1 tablespoon at a time, to the cream cheese mixture and beat well. If the icing is too runny, add more confectioners' sugar. If the icing is too thick, thin it with more pineapple juice.

to assemble the cake

PLACE one cake layer upside down on a serving plate and spread some icing on top of it. Place the other layer right side up on top of the iced lower layer. The two layers should meet perfectly. Spread the remaining icing over the top of the cake and on the sides. Serve.

WHAT IS IT AND WHERE DO I FIND IT?

CONFECTIONERS' SUGAR: Look for it in the baking section of any supermarket. It is sugar ground into a fine powder with a bit of cornstarch added as a binder. Its fine consistency allows it to soak up liquid quickly, so that icings such as this one can be made almost instantly.

blueberry buckle

Country cousin to traditional cake, this dessert is full of berries and topped with a cinnamon-sugar crust

Serves 10 to 12 ✳ *Prep time: 30 minutes* ✳ *Cooking time: 45 minutes*

INGREDIENTS

- ½ **cup (1 stick)** sweet unsalted butter, room temperature
- ¾ **cup** sugar
- 1 large egg, lightly beaten
- ½ **cup** low-fat milk
- 2 **cups** all-purpose flour
- 2 **teaspoons** baking powder
- ¼ **teaspoon** salt
- 3 **cups** blueberries
- 1 **teaspoon** lemon juice

TOPPING

- 1 **cup** firmly packed brown sugar
- ⅔ **cup** all-purpose flour
- 1½ **teaspoons** ground cinnamon
- ½ **teaspoon** ground nutmeg
- ½ **cup (1 stick)** sweet (unsalted) butter

for the cake

1. PREHEAT the oven to 375°F. Generously grease a 9-inch square or round deep-dish baking pan with vegetable oil or cooking oil spray. (A deep-dish pan has sides that are 2 inches high.)

3. PLACE the butter and sugar in a medium-size mixing bowl. Using an electric mixer, beat them together for about 3 minutes, until the mixture is smooth and creamy.

3. ADD the egg and milk to the butter mixture and stir until they are well blended.

4. COMBINE the flour, baking powder, and salt in a medium-size bowl.

5. ADD the flour mixture to the sugar-egg mixture a third at a time, stirring until they are just blended together.

6. FOLD the blueberries gently into the batter. Add the zest. Pour the batter into the pan and set it aside.

Buckles are best served warm with a dollop of whipped cream.

for the topping

1. COMBINE all of the ingredients in a medium-size bowl. Mash them together with a fork until the mixture resembles coarse meal or oatmeal. Sprinkle the mixture over the cake batter.

2. BAKE the cake for 45 minutes or until a wooden toothpick inserted into the center of it comes out clean. Serve warm.

✳ NOW WHAT?! ✳

Can other berries such as blackberries, raspberries, or strawberries be substituted?

Blueberries are traditional in this dish because they don't bleed as much as the other berries do, and they hold their shape well. Use small blueberries, called wild Maine blueberries, whenever possible—they are much tastier than the large ones.

187

peach and blackberry crumb pie

A delicious way to use up ripe peaches

Serves 6-8 ✺ *Prep time: 30 minutes* ✺ *Cooking time: 1 hour*

INGREDIENTS

- **1 unbaked 9-inch** pie shell (prepared or homemade—see page 176)
- **¼ cup** brown sugar, packed
- **1 teaspoon** cinnamon
- **½ teaspoon** ground ginger
- **¼ teaspoon** ground nutmeg
- **5 tablespoons** all-purpose flour
- **4 cups** fresh peaches, peeled and sliced; canned peaches, drained; or frozen, sliced peaches
- **3 cups** blackberries or blueberries
- **1 teaspoon** lemon zest (see page 83)
- **1 ½ tablespoons** lemon juice

CRUMB TOPPING

- **¾ cup** all-purpose flour
- **½ cup** quick oats
- **½ cup** brown sugar, firmly packed
- **⅔ cup** almonds, chopped
- **6 tablespoons** sweet unsalted butter, chilled

1. **PREHEAT** the oven to 375°F.

2. **PREPARE** the pie crust and place it in a 9-inch glass pie pan. If using a purchased pie crust, transfer it to a 9-inch glass pie pan.

3. **PLACE** the brown sugar, cinnamon, ginger, nutmeg, and flour in a large mixing bowl and stir together. Add the peaches and toss until they are well coated with the sugar-flour mixture. Gently fold in the blackberries.

4. **SPOON** the fruit mixture into the pie crust and sprinkle with the lemon zest and lemon juice.

5. In a medium-size bowl, stir together the flour, oats, brown sugar, and almonds. Add the butter and mash it with a fork until the mixture is crumbly. **SPRINKLE** the crumb mixture evenly over the fruit.

6. **BAKE** the pie for 1 hour. Remove the pan to a wire rack and cool slightly for about 15 minutes. Serve warm.

WHAT IS IT AND WHERE DO I FIND IT?

BLACKBERRIES are a joy of summer. Choose plump, glossy, deep-colored berries without hulls. (If the hulls are still attached, the berries are immature and will be very tart.) Fresh blackberries can be refrigerated for up to 2 days.

* * *

PEACHES are another glory of summer. Look for smooth, round, firm fruit that is free from blemishes and has a good white or yellow color. Avoid immature peaches—they have a washed-out look and a plastic taste. Fully ripe peaches should be refrigerated for no longer than 2 days.

* * *

UNBAKED PASTRY SHELLS can be found in the refrigerated food section of any supermarket. You can also find frozen pie crusts in the freezer section, or make your own crust using a packaged mix found in the baking ingredients section.

☀ NOW WHAT?! ☀

Which other fruits can I substitute?
Almost any summer fruit is good in a crumb pie such as this. Try blueberries instead of blackberries and nectarines instead of peaches, or a combination of peaches, nectarines, and several berries.

* * *

How do I peel a peach?
Bring a pot of water to a boil. Using a sharp knife, make an X in the base of the peach. Using a slotted spoon, lower the peach into the boiling water for no more than 1 minute. Transfer the peach to a bowl of ice water. When cool, peel the peach with your thumbs.

FIRST PERSON DISASTER

Lemon Juice Saves the Day

I love fruit pies and was getting pretty good at making one that called for sliced peaches. I had just finished slicing the peaches when the phone rang. An emergency: My daughter's ride home never showed after soccer practice. An hour later, back in the kitchen with my daughter, I started back on my pie. Too late—the peaches were all brown and soggy.

I tossed them, and we had ice cream for dessert instead. When I told a friend what happened, she told me that next time I should sprinkle lemon juice on the freshly sliced fruit, and cover with plastic wrap to keep it from turning brown.

Sarah T., Bismarck, North Dakota

quick cheesecake tart

Any combination of fruit works as a topping

Serves 6-8 ✳ *Prep time: 30 minutes* ✳ *Cooking time: 15 minutes* ✳ *Chilling time: 30 minutes*

INGREDIENTS

- **1** unbaked pie crust (prepared or homemade—see page 176), room temperature
- **1 teaspoon** flour, for dusting
- **1 package (8 ounces)** light cream cheese (see next page), softened
- **2 tablespoons** sugar
- **1 teaspoon** lemon zest (see page 83)
- **3 tablespoons** amaretto (optional, see next page)
- **1 teaspoon** almond extract (see next page)
- **1½ teaspoons** vanilla extract
- **½ pint** blueberries
- **2-3** firm peaches or nectarines, peeled and sliced, or frozen and presliced
- **½ pint** raspberries, strawberries, and blackberries

GLAZE

- **2 tablespoons** apricot preserves
- **2 tablespoons** seedless raspberry preserves

1. **PREHEAT** the oven to 450°F.

2. **DUST** the pie crust with flour and place it, flour side down, in a 9-inch tart pan with a removable bottom. Form thick sides by folding in the excess pastry instead of trimming it off. Pierce crust with fork.

3. **BAKE** the crust for 12 to 15 minutes or until it is lightly browned. (Don't worry if the crust cracks.) Set aside to cool.

4. **PLACE** the cream cheese, sugar, lemon zest, amaretto, and almond and vanilla extracts in a large bowl. Using an electric mixer, beat until blended thoroughly.

5. **SPREAD** the mixture in the cooled crust and refrigerate until it is firm, 45 minutes to 1 hour. (The tart may be prepared up to this point as much as a day in advance. Cover the tart with foil and keep it refrigerated.)

6. If using blueberries, **MOUND** them in the center of the tart. Surround them with a circle of peaches or nectarines and place raspberries and blackberries around the outside edges. Or skip the peaches and nectarines and use only berries.

7. In a small saucepan, **MELT** the preserves over low heat, stirring frequently so that they don't burn.

8. BRUSH the glaze over the fruit. Refrigerate the tart until ready to serve.

WHAT IS IT AND WHERE DO I FIND IT?

LIGHT CREAM CHEESE can be found in the dairy case of most supermarkets. It is more delicate than regular cream cheese, so it blends better with fruit and berries.

* * *

ALMOND EXTRACT is oil from the nuts dissolved in alcohol. Intensely flavorful, extracts are used in small amounts to enhance the taste of cakes and cookies. Look for them in the baking or spice section of your market.

* * *

AMARETTO is an almond-flavored liqueur that adds a lovely flavor and scent to dishes. It also makes a nice after-dinner drink, either by itself or with coffee. Amaretto can be purchased at most liquor stores.

The berries make this cheese tart lighter and fruitier than traditional cheesecake.

glossary

AL DENTE Slightly underdone with a chewy consistency. Italian for "to the tooth." A term usually applied to the cooking of pasta but also to vegetables that are not fully cooked.

BAKE To cook by free-circulating dry air in an enclosed space, such as an oven. Baking usually refers to cakes, cookies, pies, etc., as opposed to roasting, which refers to meat.

BARBECUE Technically, to cook meat using indirect heat in an enclosed space over natural woods. However, "barbecue" and "grill" have become synonymous, meaning to cook food directly over intense heat, usually out of doors using natural woods, charcoal, or gas on a grill, in an open pit or on a spit.

BASTE To pour, brush, or drizzle a liquid over whatever it is you are cooking in order to moisten it and add flavor. A bulb baster is convenient to use.

BEAT To blend or mix ingredients rapidly so that air is incorporated, resulting in a smooth, creamy mixture that has more volume.

BIND To add an agent or ingredient, such as an egg, to a dish to cement or hold the dish together.

BLANCH To plunge food briefly into boiling water in order to tenderize it or mellow its flavor. Blanching also enhances the color of vegetables.

BLEND To combine ingredients together to a desired consistency.

BOIL To heat water or other liquids to 212°F (at sea level); bubbles will form on the surface.

BONE To remove the bones from meat, poultry, fish, or game. A boning knife is a handy tool for such chores.

BRAISE To cook meat or vegetables in a small amount of liquid in a tightly closed container. This method is ideal for tougher cuts of meat, firm-fleshed fish, and numerous vegetables.

BREAD To dredge or coat food with bread crumbs.

BROIL To cook with intense heat, usually by placing under the broiling heat element in an oven. (In most ovens, the broiling heat element is on the top, the baking heat element on the bottom.) The high heat seals in juices, allowing the outside to brown but keeping the inside tender.

BROWN To cook briefly in hot fat, allowing a crust (usually brown) to form on all sides and seal in the juices. This method also enriches the flavor of the food.

CHOP To use a knife to cut up food into small uniform pieces or cubes.

CLARIFY To separate the clear, liquid part of a mixture from the solids.

CREAM To mix a softened ingredient or a combination of ingredients until well blended and completely soft. Butter and sugar are often creamed together. Remember, you can't overdo it.

CRIMP To decorate the edge of a pie crust by pinching the dough with your fingers or a fork. It is used to seal in the filling on a pie with two crusts.

CURDLE What happens when minute solids separate from the liquid in an egg or cream-based mixture due to its being heated too quickly.

CUT or **CUT IN** A pastry term meaning to mix shortening or butter with flour or other dry ingredients until the mixture resembles coarse meal. To do this, you can use two knives and cut the shortening or butter directly into the flour, or use your fingers to mix it into the flour.

DASH A very small quantity; a scant $\frac{1}{8}$ of a teaspoon.

DEGLAZE To create a sauce from the little bits of meat or poultry leftover in a pan after browning, sautéing, broiling, or roasting by adding a small amount of liquid, mixing it all together, and allowing it to boil up.

DEGREASE To remove a layer of fat from the top of a soup, sauce, or stock.

DEVEIN To remove the dark vein that runs along the back of a shrimp using a sharp knife or a special deveining tool.

DICE To cut food into small equal-size cubes, usually ranging in size from $\frac{1}{8}$ to $\frac{1}{4}$ inch.

DOLLOP A very small amount, usually a teaspoonful.

DRAIN To remove liquid or fat from food, often by placing it in a colander or strainer or on a paper towel.

DREDGE To lightly coat food, usually with flour, cornmeal, or bread crumbs. One quick way to coat food is to put the coating material in a zip-top bag, add the food to be coated, then seal the bag and shake.

DRIZZLE To slowly spatter drops of a liquid over food in a thin stream.

DUST To sprinkle very lightly with flour or sugar.

FLAKE To test the flesh of a fish to see if it is done, by breaking away a small piece or flake with a fork.

FOLD To gently incorporate one ingredient into another not by stirring or beating but by lifting from underneath with a rubber spatula.

FRY To cook food in hot fat in a skillet until brown and crisp.

GARNISH To decorate foods with fresh herbs, edible flowers, fresh vegetables, nuts, or fruit to enhance the appearance of the dish.

GRATE To rub a food against a rough surface (such as the side of a grater) to get fine shreds or tiny chunks of the food. Used for cheeses and vegetables.

GREASE To lightly coat a pan with a bit of butter, oil, or vegetable oil cooking spray to prevent cooked food from sticking.

GRILL To cook food directly over intense heat on a rack over hot coals, natural wood, or gas. See BARBECUE.

GRIND To turn a solid piece of food into fine pieces or powder by using a mortar and pestle, a food processor, or a meat grinder.

JULIENNE To cut fresh vegetables or other foods into thin, matchstick-size pieces of the same length.

KNEAD To work a finished dough until it is smooth and elastic. To use the palms of your hands on a lightly floured wooden or marbled bread board.

MARINATE To enhance the flavor and tenderize the texture of a food by placing it in a seasoned liquid, usually a combination of oil and spices and some type of acidic liquid such as vinegar, juice, or wine.

MELT To dissolve a solid or semisolid over slow heat. The term is most commonly associated with butter and chocolate.

MINCE To cut a food into very fine pieces, not larger than a $\frac{1}{8}$-inch square.

MIX To blend ingredients using a spoon or a fork.

PARBOIL To partially cook food in boiling water or broth. Similar to blanching, except the food is left in for a longer period of time when parboiling.

POACH Cooking food in a simmering liquid that does not boil. Poaching brings out the full, delicate flavor of a food.

POUND Flattening meat or poultry, often between sheets of waxed paper, using a heavy mallet or frying pan. Pounding helps tenderize meat and poultry.

PREHEAT Setting an oven or broiler to a certain temperature 10 to 15 mintues before placing food in it.

PRICK Piercing food with the tines of a fork to prevent it from bursting or rising during baking.

PURÉE Using a blender or food processor to turn cooked food into a smooth liquid, which is also called a purée.

RECONSTITUTE Rehydrating dry food by soaking it in liquid.

REDUCE Boiling a sauce to reduce its volume and intensify its flavor.

REFRESH Stopping a food from cooking by running it under cold water or plunging it into cold water.

RENDER Liquifying or leaching out the solid fat by heating. Usually done when cooking meat or poultry.

ROAST Cooking food, usually uncovered, in an enclosed space by the free circulation of dry heat.

SAUTÉ Cooking food quickly in a small amount of butter or fat over medium to high heat while turning the food frequently so that it doesn't burn.

SCALD Heating a liquid (often milk or cream) over low heat until just below its boiling point.

SHRED Cutting or tearing a food into thin strips.

SIFT Passing dry ingredients through a fine mesh strainer to remove lumps and lighten the texture (often done with flour).

SIMMER Cooking food, usually a soup or stew, over low heat so that it almost but never quite reaches a boil. Small bubbles will appear on the surface.

SLIVER Cutting a food into extra-thin strips.

SNIP Cutting herbs into small bits using scissors or kitchen shears.

STEAM Cooking food in a covered container using a small amount of boiling liquid.

STEW Cooking food slowly over relatively low heat.

STIR Mixing or blending a mixture together in a circular motion using a spoon or other implement, or, if over heat, moving food around to prevent it from burning or curdling.

STIR-FRY A cooking method developed by the Chinese which consists of quickly moving food around in a small amount of oil in a wok or frying pan. The food is lightly coated with the oil while being constantly stirred in the pan. It is essential that ingredients be cut, sliced, or otherwise prepared and ready for cooking in their proper order without any delays.

STRAIN Removing solids from liquids by pouring through a sieve, strainer, or colander.

STUFF To fill a cavity with a mixture, for example, poultry, fish, meat, vegetables.

TOAST Browning food by baking it directly under heat.

TOSS Gently mixing food by using a large spoon or fork to lift it from the bottom.

TRUSS Tying the legs and wings of poultry close to the body with string before roasting in order to preserve it in compact form and prevent the stuffing from falling out of the cavity.

WHIP Beating a food such as cream rapidly, either by hand, using a fork or a whisk, or with an electric mixer or food processor. Whipping adds a great deal of air, thereby increasing the food's volume.

WHISK Mixing sauces, dressings, eggs, and other liquids in a swift, circular motion, usually using a balloon-shaped wire instrument, also called a whisk.

ZEST The finely grated skin of a citrus fruit such as lemon, lime, or orange. When making zest, be careful not to use the bitter white pith found just underneath the surface of the skin. You can use a grater, vegetable peeler, or zester (a special tool used just to make zest) to accomplish this feat.

index

THE AUTHOR: UP CLOSE

Pamela Richards has worked as a professional chef, cookbook collaborator, and caterer. But it was as a cooking teacher to beginners that Pam found her true calling. "The trick is to explain the rules of cooking without dampening the fun of it." Who better to write **Barnes & Noble Basics** *In the Kitchen*. As she tells her students at the beginning of each semester: "Relax, if you can read, you can make anything." Pam lives in Allendale, New Jersey, with her two daughters.

Barbara J. Morgan Publisher, Silver Lining Books

Barnes & Noble Basics™
Barb Chintz Editorial Director
Leonard Vigliarolo Design Director

Barnes & Noble Basics™ *In the Kitchen*
Emily Seese Editorial Assistant
Della R. Mancuso Production Manager